Building Strong Music Programs

A Handbook for Preservice and Novice Music Teachers

Charlene Ryan

Published in partnership with
MENC: The National Association for Music Education

Rowman & Littlefield Education
Lanham • New York • Toronto • Plymouth, UK

Published in partnership with
MENC: The National Association for Music Education

Published in the United States of America
by Rowman & Littlefield Education
A Division of Rowman & Littlefield Publishers, Inc.
A wholly owned subsidiary of The Rowman & Littlefield Publishing Group, Inc.
4501 Forbes Boulevard, Suite 200, Lanham, Maryland 20706
www.rowmaneducation.com

Estover Road
Plymouth PL6 7PY
United Kingdom

British Library Cataloguing in Publication Information Available

Library of Congress Cataloging-in-Publication Data

Ryan, Charlene, 1971-
  Building strong music programs : a handbook for preservice and novice music
teachers / Charlene Ryan.
      p. cm.
  "Published in partnership with MENC: The National Association for Music
Education."
  ISBN 978-1-60709-121-9 (cloth : alk. paper) — ISBN 978-1-60709-122-6 (pbk. : alk.
paper) — ISBN 978-1-60709-123-3 (ebook)
  1. Music—Instruction and study. I. Title.
  MT1.R95 2009
  780.71'2—dc22   2009001984

∞™ The paper used in this publication meets the minimum requirements
of American National Standard for Information Sciences—Permanence of
Paper for Printed Library Materials, ANSI/NISO Z39.48-1992.
Manufactured in the United States of America.

To Matthew and Aiden:
may you always experience the joy
of music in your lives.

To Mom and Dad,
for your unfailing support.

And to Matt, for everything.

Contents

Foreword
Eugenia Costa-Giomi

Most of us started our teaching careers with the enthusiasm that a new job and long-awaited experience can bring. We were eager to meet the young faces of our students and ready to pass them our knowledge and love for music. Despite the trepidation of walking into unknown classrooms, we felt prepared for the challenges of working at a school. We believed that our education as musicians and teachers had provided us with the essential skills and knowledge that would allow us to develop focused lesson plans, set clear long-term goals for our program, and effectively guide students toward these goals. And in general, we had good reason to believe so. Through the multitude of courses we had taken and the field experiences in which we had participated, we had gained a solid preparation for working with students in the music classroom.

What we were not aware of when we started our teaching careers was that the success of our music program depended not only on what we did with the students in the classroom but also on what we did with other people outside rehearsals and lessons. We did not anticipate the amount of effort and skill needed to establish strong relationships with the school and district administration, colleagues, and parents. We did not foresee the difficulties involved in organizing and funding concerts, trips, and competitions. We did not expect to invest so much time in making our program visible in the school community. We were surprised and overwhelmed by the administrative and organizational tasks of ordering music, repairing instruments, soliciting help from parents, printing concert programs, registering students for competitions, dispensing uniforms, disseminating the achievements of students, submitting grades, booking buses, among many, many other tasks. The list of things that we had to do

besides being in front of a class seemed endless. We did not know that being a teacher required so much more than just teaching!

Charlene Ryan introduces aspiring and novice music educators to the
world of teaching. Her book provides an overview of the multiple jobs of
the music teacher as organizer, leader, fundraiser, publicist, scheduler,
and music office manager. It lists the numerous tasks that music teachers
must oversee, including some that may seem trivial or unrelated to the actual teaching of music, but that, as experienced music educators would
agree, are crucial for the smooth development of the program. The aspects
of the music programs that Ryan describes usually receive little attention
in the method classes and professional seminars attended by future music teachers. This is why this book will be a cherished resource for those
just about to start their teaching careers. It provides novice teachers with
a broad but clear list of responsibilities, and simple and practical advice
of how to go about them. This book does not intend to teach music educators how to conduct an ensemble, sequence material, or diagnose students' problems; these skills are developed throughout years of training
and are at the core of effective teaching. Rather, this book reminds teachers of the multitude of administrative and organizational tasks of which
they are also responsible and suggests efficient ways to fulfill them.

The advice that Ryan provides is wise and practical. She highlights the
importance of recruiting help from many sources, students, parents, community members, and other teachers and suggests ways to do so. She iden-
tifies tasks that can be delegated to others, activities that enrich the social
lives of music students, noncurricular programs that contribute to the
growth of school music, and events that can make the music program more
visible in the community. She provides tips about how to make students'
achievements known, create a welcoming classroom for learners and teachers, and communicate with parents and the rest of the school. She suggests
ways to approach budgets, grading, recruitment, special needs of students,
and other critical aspects of the school music program. In summary, this
book provides beginning teachers with valuable knowledge and ideas.

It takes effective teaching skills to develop musicianship in our students.
But it also takes superb organizational skills to build strong music programs. Ryan's book addresses the latter in a simple, friendly, and practical
way. I hope that preservice and novice teachers will take a few short hours
to read this book and learn how to save themselves from the long hours of
stress and frustration often associated with the first years of teaching.

Eugenia Costa-Giomi, PhD
Professor, music and human learning
Buttler School of Music
University of Texas–Austin

Acknowledgments

To my former students at McGill University in Montreal and my current students at the Berklee College of Music in Boston—thank you for your great questions, concerns, and issues that have fueled my drive to write this book. I hope that future students will benefit from your uncertainties!

To Clive Austin, headmaster at West Point Grey Academy in Vancouver—thanks for being the kind of principal that every music teacher hopes for. You afforded me the opportunity, support, and freedom to implement many of the strategies noted in this book. To my former colleagues, students, and parents at WPGA, my gratitude—I learned so much from you.

There are three particularly special teachers—Sister Kathrine Bellamy and Sister Celine Veitch of St. John's, Newfoundland, and Professor Gwen Beamish of the University of Western Ontario—who helped shape my beliefs about what good teaching should be. I will be forever grateful to you for your wise and caring ways. Extended thanks also go out to all of my former school and college teachers, each of whom have contributed to my growth and development.

My gratitude and thanks to those who read draft versions and provided valuable feedback. In particular I would like to acknowledge Allan Anderson of the Canadian Music Educators Association and Dr. Sandra Nicolucci at Boston University—thank you for sharing your time and expertise in reading my manuscript and providing valuable suggestions and comments. I am very grateful. Similarly, Jason Freeland provided thoughtful comments, encouragement, and suggestions, which were a great benefit to the book.

To Fran Ponick, thank you for your enthusiasm and encouragement and for sharing my vision of this book from the outset. I am very grateful to Sue Rarus, Linda Brown, Pat Woofter, and the team at MENC for your support, assistance, careful eye and suggestions. Special thanks are likewise due to Paul Cacciato, Lynda Phung, Maera Stratton, and the team at Rowman & Littlefield Education for your editing, proofing, preparation, and production of this book. You have been each been wonderful groups to work with.

To my supervisor, professor, mentor, and dear friend, Eugenia Costa-Giomi at the University of Texas at Austin—thank you for your encouragement, advice, candor, and friendship.

To my parents, who did not grow up with music education, but who saw that all of their children did, who spent countless hours listening to us practice and perform, driving us to and from lessons and rehearsals, competitions and performances, who allowed us the freedom to pursue any interests and school courses we wished, and who believed that music was an important and valuable path to pursue professionally—thank you again. You are an inspiration. To my brothers and sisters, Marie, Pius, Aiden, and Michael, who have always believed in me, and who put up with the seemingly endless hours of practicing—thank you.

To my husband, Matt, for your unfailing support, for your belief in and encouragement of this project from its very conception, and for always being there for me—I am so blessed to be sharing this life with you. To my children, Matthew and Aiden, thank you for your patience, love, and beautiful smiles through Mama's long hours at the computer. I love my little family more than words can say.

Preface

Music education as a profession requires a unique combination of high-level skills in both music and pedagogy. Most music teachers, indeed most musicians, begin training for their careers well before adolescence, and many from early childhood. Their education is then continued at the post-secondary level, with a focus not only on developing a high level of musicianship, but also on learning a wide range of skills pertaining to the teaching of young musicians. Music-teacher training programs in North America usually take between four and six years to complete, after which graduates must become certified to teach by the province or state in which they plan to work. Despite the breadth and depth of these programs, many music teachers graduate unprepared for the complexities of the role they aspire to fill. While musical skills and pedagogical knowledge may be in place, students often lack an understanding of the multiple roles of today's music teachers.

Unlike its so-called "academic" counterparts, such as math, science, and English, music education has endured a veritable roller-coaster ride in the public school system. It seems to move from being a "frill" to being the pride of the school and back again, depending on the educational agenda of a given school administration and/or government. As a result, music teachers now find themselves in positions in which their teaching must go beyond the classroom or ensemble room. Today's music teachers need to educate the wider school community about the value of music education in children's lives. This includes educating parents, other teachers, principals, school boards, and governments. In addition to the challenge of balancing a high-quality music curriculum and high-level music performances, music teachers must be strong and vocal advocates for their chosen field; they must be adept fund-raisers; and they must be good businesspeople if their programs are to thrive in the reality of today's schools.

While many fine books have been written about the various techniques and skills required to be a qualified music teacher, what is missing up to this point is one that focuses on the building and maintenance of a music program within the constructs of a school environment. Program building is an essential, unavoidable, and often time-consuming component of every music teacher's job. However, students are rarely well prepared for this prospect during their teacher-training years. As a result, many music teachers spend the early part of their careers learning by trial and error, and not making effective use of the resources available to them. The many facets and stresses that come with the realities of the job are, unfortunately, reflected in the high rate of burnout among young music teachers within the first few years on the job.

It is well known in educational circles that music and the other arts often suffer first and most from government shifts and budgetary constraints. However, music teachers who have built strong, respected programs can often weather such changing times. It is therefore critical for music teachers to have the knowledge and tools with which to develop such a program and to build a community of support within their school. It is relatively easy for administrators to cut an individual teacher or program, but much less easy to justify such cuts to a community of unhappy parents and teachers.

This book is designed for music education majors nearing the end of their undergraduate training, who have already developed most of the skill sets of a music teacher. It is a resource that music teachers will continue to use throughout the early part of their careers. The ideas and projects are relevant to all levels of music teaching from preschool through high school, though some will clearly be more appropriate for one level than another. Student assignments are provided at the end of each chapter and students are given the option to focus their assignments on the particular school level at which they intend to teach. Since many young music teachers find that their preferred teaching level does not become clear until they are well into their first year of teaching, this broad range of questions provides them with the flexibility to adapt this book to their changing needs.

The ideas presented here have developed out of my experience as a music teacher from preschool through high school levels, from my reflections upon the many things I wish someone had told me before my first day at work, from conversations with fellow music teachers, from the many wonderful questions and concerns of my university students, and from the absence of and need for a resource that helps young music teachers better understand and be better prepared for their role as a music teacher. My hope is that this book will round out every student's music-teacher training by preparing them for the many aspects of the job that have little to do with clarinet fingerings, choral balance, or singing game repertoire, and more to do with building strong and enduring music programs.

Chapter 1

Your First Job

Music education is an exciting, exhausting, and ultimately rewarding profession. Few others allow you to simultaneously practice what you love to do while instilling a similar passion in children and adolescents. At all levels of schooling, there are many opportunities for developing creative and vibrant classes and nurturing budding young musicians.

Landing your first job as a professional music educator is a wonderful landmark event that is both exciting and somewhat daunting. Now is the time to put all the skills and knowledge of your college training into practice. What you need now are the practical tools with which to effectively achieve your goals within the constructs of the school environment. While preparing for and implementing your curriculum, you must also strive to create your place, and your voice, within the existing school community, and to carve out an important position for music education within that community. This book is all about strategies you can use in creating, maintaining, promoting, and supporting a strong, vibrant music program in your school.

This first chapter deals with some key initial steps young teachers should take when assigned a new teaching position. If you are lucky, you will have an entire summer to prepare, but invariably some teachers end up with mere weeks, even days, to get ready for the start of the year. In either case, as much preparation as can be done before beginning your new position can help you immensely when Day 1 rolls around. Learning about the school, program, curriculum, protocol, schedule, regulations, community, values, and expectations prior to the start of the school year will enable you to effectively plan for the year ahead.

This chapter is not a step-by-step guide to preparing for your first job, and it is by no means exhaustive. The suggestions presented here are meant to guide your overall preparation and thinking about a new school and new position. The chapters that follow provide a wealth of ideas with which to grow and nurture that program such that it is strong, resilient, valued, and supported by staff, students, and the wider school community.

WHAT CAME BEFORE . . .

One of the most important tasks for new teachers is in finding out where their students are with respect to musical understandings and skills. This information will guide repertoire choices, curriculum plans, performance decisions, and indeed, what you do in class on Day 1. A little advance knowledge about the existing program will help you immeasurably in understanding (a) what to expect from your students and (b) what they, and the rest of the school community, will expect from you.

Examine any available concert programs—you may be able to track them down through the main secretary or through the music department files. These will provide some information about the level and style of repertoire that students have recently been working on. They will also inform you as to the details of school concerts—the typical format, their placement within the school year, the grades and groups that take part, the length of the program, and the type of material presented.

Inquire as to the existence of concert video recordings (many music departments record their performances). These can provide even more information since they allow you to see and hear the level at which students are performing, the size and makeup of the ensembles, how the concert environment is arranged, and what the students typically wear. They can also provide you with cues about the makeup of the student body and school community, and the support for its music program.

Music teachers who have worked to build a strong school program hope that this program continues to flourish once they have moved elsewhere. To help smooth the transition between teachers, some incumbent teachers leave key information prepared for their successor. Check to see whether your predecessor has left an information packet for you—perhaps on your desk, in your mailbox, or with the main office.

If you are hired before the end of the school year, you may be able to arrange a meeting or a phone conversation with the teacher you are replacing (assuming he or she is leaving on positive terms). Details pertaining to previous years' curriculum, repertoire, ensembles, extracurricular rehearsals, and budget matters can be very helpful coming from the person who has been implementing them before you. While you may not want to continue along the identical path that your predecessor established, knowing what the program was like under his or her direction will help you enormously in planning how to proceed.

EXPLORE

Take some time to explore and consider your new teaching space, facilities, and equipment. How will you prepare the room for students' learning? How will you orient the chairs and/or risers for optimal space usage? What inspirational and educational materials would you like for the walls, and where can you place them? What equipment do you have? What repertoire does the department own? Where are the repertoire and other resources stored, and is this space appropriate? Are the existing octavos and instrumental parts organized or are there stacks needing to be filed? Do you have bulletin boards? If not, do you want them and how can you arrange to have them for September? What instruments do you have? Where are they stored? Do they need repairs? Are there other instruments that you feel are essential to the development of your program and, if so, is it possible to have them this year? Does the school own a current elementary music series? What recordings are available?

Learning about your teaching environment and materials is a critical first step in preparing for the job. Knowing what space and resources you have can have major implications for the program you run. The more you learn about and become comfortable with your new space and materials before school begins, the better positioned you will be to take ownership of the program before students arrive.

FINDING REPERTOIRE

One of the most exciting, and potentially overwhelming, tasks for novice music teachers is the selection of repertoire. You will likely have learned some school repertoire throughout your college training and may even recall some selections from your own years in school. Still, you may find that more resources are required in finding appropriate repertoire for the various classes and ensembles for which you are now responsible (this is particularly challenging when you have little or no information about the current level of your students). Aside from hitting the local music store to browse through endless reams of repertoire, there are a number of valuable resources available to you.

First, you should begin attending school concerts and music festivals while still in college. These events are invaluable sources of information about the level of playing in a variety of school programs, common problems across ensembles, effective conducting styles, and repertoire. Write comments in the program next to titles about style, difficulty level, appeal, text, range, solos, and any unique aspects of the selections, and keep a collection of these programs in a folder for future reference. Contact festival associations to ask for recommended and required repertoire lists. These usually contain excellent, tried-and-true selections that will start you off on solid footing. Recordings of community child and youth choirs, bands, and orchestras are another excellent source of potential repertoire. Information about purchasing these recordings is often available on the ensembles' websites.

Music stores that supply school repertoire are good sources of information. They often have copies of festival lists available, and many host choral reading sessions over the summer months. Reading sessions are great opportunities to try out new repertoire with other musicians, to meet other music teachers in your area, and to take home a selection of individual octavos to mull over. While reading sessions are not as common for band and orchestra repertoire, it has become relatively common for publishers to supply merchants with CDs of new repertoire. These are typically available in-house for music teachers to listen to when making their repertoire decisions. Publishers often send these CDs and free octavos of choral repertoire with their representatives for distribution in the marketplace at music teacher conferences. Some publishers and distributors also contain demo MP3s directly on their websites.

Perhaps the best source of information on good repertoire is word of mouth. Talk with music teachers you know, and keep in touch with your college classmates and professors. Through personal connections you will be able to garner details about appropriate and effective repertoire for various occasions, ensemble types, grades, and voicings.

Assuming you are hired with a little advance notice, you will need to make some purchases of repertoire prior to the start of the school year. There may be material already available at the school that you would like to use, but beware of re-using selections that have been played or sung in the last year or two. If you do know what has been done recently, then it is best to steer clear of those selections at the beginning. If you feel you have a good sense of where the students are musically, you should select enough pieces to get you through at least the first couple of months, if not through to December. This allows you to have an overall plan for the term whereby you can learn and prepare the material in advance of Day 1, enabling you to start the year off on solid footing.

Some teachers prefer to select only enough material for September, or even just the first couple of rehearsals (in which case you might actually revisit some selections from last year), so that they can get a feel for their students' needs, abilities, and interests before finalizing decisions about term repertoire and material for the rest of the year. This is a particularly good plan when new teachers have little or no information about the existing program—in which case it is sometimes best to start with music that is low cost or free. Music that the department owns, music from the public domain library, and music that is borrowed from another school or music teachers' association are good choices for this purpose.

A final note about purchasing music—always allow for extra time for it to arrive, in case the selections you want are not currently in stock. Be sure to give yourself enough time to learn the music and to work out an effective teaching strategy before bringing it to your students.

CONCERTS

Concerts are a regular component of practically every school music program at every level. They are the primary source of information the school community often has about the music program—and judgments are often made about teachers and programs based on these events. When you are new to a position, there are some key questions that you should ask either the principal, fellow music teachers, or the outgoing music teacher that will facilitate your effective planning for concerts.

How many concerts regularly happen each year and during what months do they take place? Are they exclusively music concerts or are other programs, such as drama, also showcased? Are all students meant to participate, or just the performing ensembles? How long do they traditionally run? Where have they traditionally been held? Are there restrictions as to what repertoire may be performed? Many public schools will not permit sacred music to be performed at school concerts or, conversely, will request that sacred music from a variety of faiths be presented on a given December program. Since repertoire choices are made during the summer months or, at the latest, in September, you will need to know relatively early what expectations, requirements, and restrictions surround school concerts so that you can make appropriate decisions in this regard.

CURRICULUM

Curriculum guides are usually examined during the teacher-training years, and many are based on, or closely linked to, the National Standards

for Music Education. If this is not the case in your school, or if you plan
to teach in a different state or province than where you studied, you will
want to spend some time, preferably before your first interview, learning
about expectations that the school will have for potential new hires. You
will want to familiarize yourself with the National Standards as well, if
you have not already done so during your college training.

Consider how the curriculum guide fits with your hopes and plans for
the program, and formulate a solid rationale for the decisions you make.
Does the curriculum guide specify required or recommended texts or series you should be familiar with? If so, does your school own them, have
they been used in previous years, and how do they match your ideas?
Curriculum guides are intended to maintain a standard of learning across
schools and across teachers in a given school. Be sure to familiarize yourself with this important resource.

Once armed with the pertinent information about curriculum requirements, performance expectations and levels, and previous program focuses, you will need to plan the year ahead for each grade and ensemble.
These plans will undoubtedly change somewhat throughout the course of
the year as you get to know your students, their level and interests, and
the school environment better. With time and experience, you will learn
how long various lessons, skills, and repertoire selections take for students at different levels to learn. Nevertheless, you will want to have an
overall picture of the year ahead clear in your mind, and on paper, before
it all begins. Without knowing where you are going it is very difficult to
know where to begin or to achieve a sense of cohesion and direction. Using the curriculum guide, you can organize a curriculum that leads students smoothly and logically from one school year into the next.

ASSESSMENT

A major component of any well-planned curriculum is a well-structured
system of assessment. This will help you keep track of students' progress
and/or difficulties and determine whether the goals of your curriculum
have been met. It is important to learn the expectations of the school with
respect to assessment and to decide upon a plan with which you feel comfortable. This must be done before your first meeting with students. They
and their parents should be fully informed as to how grades will be for-
mulated in your class—this will avoid any misconceptions and any potential surprises come report time.

It is essential that you develop a fair, consistent, and regular system of
grading that primarily assesses student achievement in skill and concept
areas. Since ensemble and group work is a regular component of music

education, effective participation is also typically included in grading schemes. However, with perhaps the exception of the early primary grades, it is generally unwise to base grades solely on participation. In nonmusic classes, students are assessed on their grasp of the course material. This focus should be the same in music if it is to be taken seriously as a course in which effort, growth, and learning are expected. Since your music curriculum will undoubtedly involve learning outcomes, your assessment plan should address how those outcomes have been met.

You will want to inquire also as to the school's policies and expectations with respect to grading and reporting. What has been done in the past? Are some of your courses considered extracurricular, and therefore ungraded? For courses that are graded, how is this done—with a number, a letter, or a comment (e.g., satisfactory/unsatisfactory)? What are the benchmarks or criteria for these grades? When are reports given to parents? Ask for a copy of the school report card to find out what criteria you must address.

It is important to find out whether you are required to write a comment for each student. Many private schools, in particular, require individual comments from every teacher for every student they teach. Such a practice can provide an opportunity for you to give specific feedback on individual students. However, it can also take a considerable amount of time. Find out in advance so that you will schedule your time accordingly. Even if individual reports are not required, some music teachers like to prepare a paragraph or two for each grade or course summarizing students' progress and performance throughout the term, which can be inserted into the report card. This approach is a great way to keep parents up-to-date on what their children are learning in music class, while requiring minimal time on the part of the teacher.

BUDGET

Starting a new job—particularly your first—holds many exciting possibilities. However, before planning any events or purchases it is important to learn exactly what your music budget can support. This can vary greatly from school to school, even within the same district. Ask the former teacher, principal, or school accountant what is available for your program and, if possible, to see a breakdown of how this budget has been used in previous years.

Inquire about fund-raising—what has been done in the past, what the expectations and policies are, how the school community responds to such efforts, how much money is typically raised, and how it has been used. Are there certain ensembles or programs that frequently conduct a substantial amount of fund-raising? This can happen—especially for travel to festivals, field trips, uniforms, or guest clinicians. If you have the opportunity to speak with your predecessor, much of this information can be gleaned from him or her. If not, the principal, chair of finance, and/or accountant can help you. Without knowing up front what funds you have to work with, it can be difficult to make decisions about many components of your program.

CLASSROOM MANAGEMENT

Effective classroom management is essential for all teachers, but none more so than the music teacher. The absence of desks and individual seatwork and the presence of musical instruments make this a unique teaching and learning environment. Without effective tools for guiding student behavior, music rooms can quickly deteriorate into chaos.

What are the expectations for classroom management at your school? Are there certain strategies that are used throughout the entire school; do certain behaviors result in automatic visits with the principal or vice-principal? These questions can often be answered by colleagues, whom you will undoubtedly meet in the weeks leading up to the start of the school year when teachers are busy getting their classrooms and courses ready.

Once you have learned a little about the school's policies in this regard, you will want to spend some time developing a set of simple guidelines for your own classes that you can discuss with each class on the first day. Music teachers sometimes feel reluctant to implement management techniques, in fear that it may turn students off from participation in music education. Your guidelines should be thought of as a means to effectively interact in class so that music making and learning can be achieved by all.

SPECIAL NEEDS

With greater awareness and knowledge of brain functioning and how we learn, students with special learning needs are now identified younger and more accurately than ever before. This is wonderful news for the students and the teachers who work with them. Without such identification and knowledge, it would be difficult to know how to help special needs students achieve at their full potential in your class.

You should make it a point to find out which of your students require extra support and what you can do to facilitate their learning and participation in music. Some special needs may not be particularly relevant to the music classroom, while others will require careful consideration and sometimes adaptation of lesson plans and materials. It is best if you can have some awareness of these needs before teaching your first class. Otherwise you may find yourself in an uncomfortable or difficult situation that could easily have been avoided with a little forethought.

Talk to your school guidance counselor or, if possible, school psychologist regarding the classes you teach. They should be able to provide some information about students with special needs in your classes, as well as to offer particular strategies for helping those students to succeed. Some students may require Individualized Education Plans (IEPs) that account for their particular abilities and adapt the curriculum and assessment plans accordingly. Again, the guidance counselor or school psychologist should have the necessary information in this regard.

At the elementary and middle school levels, classroom teachers may also be able to provide some support and assistance with respect to identified students in their classes. Some special needs students will have teaching assistants who work with them some or all of the time, and some special needs students may only be mainstreamed for certain classes, such as music. It is essential that you find ways to help all your students succeed in music class, making the necessary adjustments to your teaching strategies to accommodate the needs of all.

LAST-MINUTE HIRES

In an ideal world, you will have signed your contract at the end of the previous school year, giving you ample time to learn about the school, the community, and the music program. However, invariably there will be principals scrambling to hire teachers the week (or day) before school starts. This can happen in cases in which teachers get sick or need to take a last-minute leave, spouses get transferred to work in a different location, or teachers take early retirement. Whatever the reason, if you have not been hired by the beginning of August do not despair. It is still possible that a position will come your way. The question is how to prepare for a new position when school starts next week?

During your job search process, you can start preparing for any possible scenarios that you might find yourself in. If you are a choral teacher, for example, familiarize yourself with repertoire for a variety of choral ensembles and levels so that you can make some quick decisions if need be. If you are an elementary specialist, familiarize yourself with a variety of common music education series—perhaps through your college's music education department or library, or through the publishers themselves. Information from sales representatives is available on the individual publishers' websites—they can send you promotional materials about their series. It may not be the same as actually browsing through the materials, but it will at least familiarize you with how each series and the lessons within them are organized.

The school where you ultimately get hired may or may not own a series or have the budget to purchase one, but familiarizing yourself with how they are put together can be beneficial in guiding your thinking about lesson planning, and give you good ideas for material and activities. Make a plan for how, ideally, you would approach designing a curriculum across the elementary grades that would provide a comprehensive music education for your students. Your ideal plan can always be adjusted to the particular teaching situation in which you find yourself, and having a plan prepared will certainly ease your last-minute transition into a new school.

No matter what your area of specialization or which kinds of jobs you have applied for, it is absolutely essential that you become familiar with the National Standards for Music Education (in the United States) or Concepts and Skills: Achieving Musical Understanding (in Canada), and the standards and/or curriculum guidelines for the state(s) or province(s) where you are seeking work. These documents, often available online, can help guide your planning by directing you to expectations that you should have for students at the end of each school level. While you are still waiting to be hired, you can strategize how to incorporate all the standards into a well-rounded curriculum no matter where you are hired. You will undoubtedly need to make some adjustments to your plans once you know the specifics of your program, but they are an excellent place to start whether or not you have advance notice of your position.

During the waiting process, try to learn a little about the school communities where you have applied for positions. Do the schools have solid existing music programs? Are they new programs? Floundering programs? What is the cultural makeup of the community? How might this affect your curriculum plans, your ensemble offerings, and your repertoire choices? Are the schools large or small, and what grades do they encompass? Is there one music teacher or many? A lot of schools have websites now, so it is relatively easy to learn about the school, its programs, teachers, and community. Whatever knowledge you can gather in advance about a potential position will serve to strengthen your job interview and your ultimate entry into the job, even if it is at the last minute.

Aside from any anticipatory preparation, what then are the most important things to focus on when you find out today that you start work on Monday? The two most important things you can do are to (a) prepare your first class for each grade or course and then (b) prepare your teaching space. These two steps will help you to both look and feel like you are starting on solid footing.

Even if plans for the rest of the year are still very much up in the air, your first classes must give the impression of a confident, competent, organized, and engaging teacher. So use the time available to you to get these classes ready. It will help a lot if you have done some of the legwork suggested above before you are hired, but even if you haven't, you can still put together excellent first lessons that give an initial taste of the kind of program you intend to lead.

Once your first classes are planned, direct your attention to your teaching space. It is absolutely essential that your students enter a room that is organized and attractive, ready for them to work, sing, play, and learn. If the room is disorganized, you will appear disorganized—not the first impression you want to give. A messy room does not give the impression of a place to work and will make it difficult for students to focus, so giving some of your limited preparation time to readying your space is necessary to starting the year off well.

Keep in mind that, even if you are hired at the last minute, you still need to fill in all the details discussed earlier in the chapter relatively early in the year. This means that your first few weeks, in particular, will be very busy. You still need to plan your curriculum, learn about your budget, resources, repertoire, and instruments; you still need to select teaching materials, order music, and find out the when, where, and who surrounding the first school concert. However, you need to be careful not to let this steep learning curve interfere with your preparation and implementation of excellent classes.

How you start the year—the initial impression that you give to students and colleagues—can establish your reputation in the school and last long after all the details have finally been set in place. So work on filling in the gaps when you can find time, but not at the expense of planning the immediate needs of your program. The first term will be hectic, no doubt, but once you have caught up, assuming you have focused on your students and classes from the start, things will settle into a more normal busyness in January.

SUMMARY

Landing your first job as a professional music educator is a wonderful and exciting event. After so many years of practice and study you are finally in the position to put your passion and skill to the test, to bring your love of music to a new generation of students. New music teachers bring a wealth of energy, enthusiasm, and fresh ideas to the classroom and to the profession—they keep music education alive and well. The ideas in this book will, hopefully, provide some food for thought and perhaps spark some flames that may result in the development and growth of even more exceptional and strong music programs in the coming years.

This book is filled with ideas for making your program a success. Some of the ideas are straightforward and practical, others require more effort and creativity; some would work well in one situation and not at all in another. Not all the suggestions provided here should be taken on in any given position, and certainly not all in the same year. It is important to pace yourself, to pick the strategies that can be applied easily in your first year, to work with those that seem most essential to your program's immediate needs, and to have some strategies that are part of a slightly longer-range plan—say, over your first three to five years. A strong, successful program takes time to build, so it is important to be realistic about what can be achieved in a given year.

You cannot do everything, at least, not all at once, and not by yourself. Many music teachers try to fill every void they see, using every waking moment working on various aspects of their programs. Often, these tireless efforts result in admirable music programs, but at the expense of the teacher's health, happiness, career, and quality of life. It is absolutely essential that you take time to live outside your job, that you maintain your own personal support network, that you keep a balanced approach to managing your program, and that you accept and ask for help when needed. By doing so, you can not only build the strong, successful music program that you envision, but you can be a part of making that program thrive throughout a long and prosperous career.

Chapter 2

Friends and Allies

A solid group of supporters can be the driving force behind a successful school music program. Building strong relationships with colleagues, parents, administrators, and others, both within and outside the school community, is essential to your success. These people, individually and collectively, can ease your workload, assist with finances, and promote your music program within the school and throughout the community. Without them, even the best-laid programs can collapse under the threat of program cuts.

Successful music educators understand that a strong support network is a vital component of a good program, not just a fortunate supplement to one. As with any other element of a good program, these connections must be built and nurtured in order to work to the program's best advantage. This chapter, therefore, focuses on establishing and maintaining positive links with the friends and allies that every good music teacher should have.

WITHIN THE SCHOOL

Collegiality

Music teachers are among the busiest people in their schools. In addition to regular school hours, rehearsals often take up early morning hours, recess, lunch, and after-school hours. It's the kind of work ethic that's great for building students' skills, but can interfere with your opportunities to interact effectively with colleagues.

Make some time, however limited it may be, to socialize with colleagues. Go to the staff room. Sit. Have a coffee and a chat. Ask for colleagues' input and advice; discuss ideas and concerns. As a new teacher, building positive, friendly relationships with your colleagues can help you to develop a support system, both on a personal and on a professional level. It can also help to develop a greater comprehension of the school environment and its traditions.

Talking with more established teachers can give you a sense of how involved parents are in the school, as well as how much importance the school community places on academics, athletics, and the arts. It may also provide valuable information about individuals or classes that affects students' behavior and achievement in your class. The fact that a particular class may be experiencing serious behavioral issues, or that the sixth graders have been pouring all their energy into science fair projects, can affect their participation and focus in your classes or rehearsals.

Additionally, through social interaction with colleagues you may be able to garner assistance with various musical endeavors. For instance, the primary grade teachers might be delighted to help their class plan and make simple costumes or props for their upcoming musical production. They might even help students rehearse lines or practice songs. The more comfortable colleagues are with you as a person, the more comfortable they will be in helping you as a fellow teacher. And the more teachers know about you and your program, the more likely they will be to support your programs and initiatives.

Musical Teachers

Surprise your students by inviting their favorite English, physics, and social studies teachers to join them for a few selections in band, orchestra, or choir, to demonstrate their skills in guitar class, or to take a small role in the school musical. Talk to your colleagues to find out who plays an instrument, if not currently then perhaps when they were in school, and uncover who the singers are. You probably have colleagues who are currently involved in music—singing in a community or church choir, playing the guitar at campfire sing-alongs, or playing a drum set in a rock band on Saturday afternoons.

Invite these teachers to contribute to your program by participating in a concert or class, by encouraging students to participate in music classes and ensembles, or by simply speaking positively to students about their own music education and musical life. Children and adolescents enjoy learning that adults they respect and admire enjoy some of the same activities that they do, and that music learning now can impact upon the rest of their lives in a very positive way. A strong case is made for the importance of music education when nonmusic teachers are open about its positive contribution to their lives.

Across the Curriculum

Many curricular areas can be greatly enhanced with music. For instance, awareness of the musical traditions of different cultures can contribute greatly to students' interest in and knowledge of social studies. Songs, chants, compositions, and musical productions can all center around literary studies. The properties of sound production, tuning, and chord structure are all fodder for high school physics. And second-language learning is greatly enhanced through the use of song. In fact, most subject areas can be linked in some way to the study of music.

Talk with grade or subject coordinators, even individual teachers, about ways that you may be able to support their curriculum, while still meeting your own curricular needs. Most teachers will be enthusiastic about such support as it helps to bring students' understanding to a deeper and potentially more meaningful level. It also connects subject areas in a way that makes sense to students, fostering awareness that no subject is an isolated area of study but rather a very specific means of examining material.

Such an approach not only supports other teachers' curriculum, it also highlights music education and makes it an obvious, relevant component of education as a whole. In addition, it brings the music program to the attention of students not currently involved and allows you the opportunity to interact with potentially interested individuals. Providing support for other teachers can result in increased support of your program initiatives on the part of your colleagues. No teacher is an island—supporting your colleagues can help build bridges for yourself and your program.

Music Colleagues

Is there more than one music teacher in your school? If so, it is a good idea to get to know your new colleagues and establish some positive relationships as soon as possible. These are the people with whom you will be working closely, sharing resources and students, and ultimately advancing the same cause within your school. It is essential to the overall health of the music program that music teachers within a school support each other and work cooperatively together.

When music colleagues do not get along, it causes tension for everyone—most especially the students—and makes for an unpleasant and stressful work environment. It is important to start off on the right foot with your colleagues. They can help ease your transition into the school, give you a heads-up about certain issues in the school, provide advice about dealing with various school personalities, and answer all sorts of questions that arise in your first days and months.

Fine Arts Department

You do not have to work alone as an advocate for music education. In many schools there are fine arts colleagues who face many of the same challenges as you. It can be beneficial to collaborate with the other music, drama, dance, and visual art instructors, to work together in support of each other and of your respective fields. Chances are good that any difficulties you may be experiencing with respect to a lack of support, time, or funding for your programs are difficulties that the other arts teachers are also experiencing.

By forming a Fine and Performing Arts Department you will be surrounding yourself with individuals with similar interests facing similar challenges. There is a certain truth to the old adage that there is strength in numbers. A group of like-minded teachers can work together as a unified front to promote arts education throughout the entire school, which can be much more effective—and less lonely—than going it alone.

Physical Education and Drama Departments

Extracurricular school time is limited. There are only five school days each week and most extracurricular activities take place before 5:30 p.m. In any given school there are generally multiple athletic, artistic, and academic activities vying for these limited slots of time. Students often find themselves in a position of having to choose between the basketball team, the school play, and the jazz band because of overlapping schedules. While students may still have to make some choices in order not to be overloaded, teachers can help alleviate some stress and ensure that those who want to be part of their extra-curricular ensemble or team can do so.

Before school starts in September, organize a meeting of all teachers responsible for scheduling extracurricular activities, teams, or groups. Ask them to come equipped with preferred time slots or, in the case of competitive sports, game days, and then work together to form a schedule with a minimum number of overlaps. This may require some concessions on everyone's part. For example, you may have to have one-hour practices instead of ninety minutes so that 3:00-to-4:00 and 4:00-to-5:00 time slots may be available for various activities. Or, perhaps some early morning or lunch-hour practices or rehearsals are possible.

It is important to promote a collegial atmosphere, and remind everyone that the goal is to do what is best for the students. In too many schools the physical education coaches and the arts teachers are near-enemies, vying for student time. It is much better to foster an environment that is flexible and beneficial for everyone. Such a system will help ensure that the star basketball/hockey/soccer/volleyball player who is also a fantastic trumpeter/bassist/tenor and the student who needs physical activity but also loves to sing gets to do both. Note: It is best to reserve this strategy for your second year in a school—once you have gotten to know your colleagues and built a relationship with them.

The Principal and Vice Principal

It goes without saying that it is important to be on good terms with your school administrators. But music teachers need to take it one step further and make principals and vice principals their allies. If you view your administrators as respected colleagues, you may feel more comfortable in being open about your ideas, needs, questions, and concerns. Remember that you and your administrators ultimately want the same thing—a high-quality education for the students.

Once you develop a professional, friendly relationship with your principal, you'll be in a better position to discuss innovations and strategies for further growth, as well as the successes and achievements of your students. You will feel more comfortable discussing issues of concern that are affecting your program, and you will be in a position to develop in your administrators an understanding of your approach to teaching and the contribution your program is making to the overall life of the school.

The more the school leaders know about your program and its strengths, and the more they like and respect you as a colleague, the more likely it will be that you get the respect and support you need, and that your administrators will stand up for you and your department in times of crisis.

The Custodian

A positive relationship with school custodians is essential. They can ease your life considerably when it comes to preparing venues for performance and transporting equipment, as well as the day-to-day maintenance of your teaching and practice space. Administering a music program with its chairs, stands, microphones, risers, instruments, and other equipment is no small job. If you want to get things done it is imperative that you get along well with those in a position to help.

Be polite, friendly, and respectful; thank your custodians for their help and compliment them on a job well done. Call individuals by name, get to know them a little, and treat them as the valued staff members that they are. And always keep in mind that you and your colleagues could not do your jobs if those that take care of the building did not do theirs.

Secretaries

Secretaries play a very important role in the life of the school. They keep track of student reports, school records, archives, and activities, and the comings and goings of students, classes, groups, teams, teachers, and administrators. They often are responsible for the preparation and copying of concert programs and other printed materials, they have contact information for everyone involved with the school, and they are typically the first point of contact for parents and visitors.

There are many ways that school secretaries can make life easier for you—from scheduling meetings with the principal to tracking down students to preparing print materials. They are important people with whom to be on good terms. Most importantly, do not "pull rank" on your secretaries. Their valuable role in the school should neither be underestimated nor taken for granted. Bad feelings created at the outset can cause much difficulty for you over time. Best to start things off on the right foot, and then keep it that way!

PARENTS

Parent Committee

A coalition of music-friendly parents can be your strongest ally in promoting music education. If your school does not already have a parent committee or booster club, you might consider making it a priority to organize one. Start early in the year by sending out a newsletter that outlines upcoming musical events and announces the first meeting of the Music Parents' Committee. Extend an open invitation for parents to meet over coffee and chat with you before delving into the role and purpose of the committee. Don't let the meeting go on for too long, and don't require parents to meet too frequently as a group. Parents, like teachers, are busy people for whom time is precious. Restricting the length and frequency of meetings will encourage them to become active members.

Make a list of everyone's e-mail and mailing addresses, phone numbers, and the names and grades of their children. Provide a list of jobs that parents can sign up for—you should have both the job list and the contact sheet typed up soon after the meeting, and copies distributed to all committee members so that they can coordinate events, activities, and small-group meetings to achieve specific tasks (this can help avoid unnecessary full-group meetings).

The main roles of the parent body are to help with administrative aspects of the program and to be a ready-made advocacy group. For example, much of the fund-raising can be organized by parents. Maintaining the music library and other resources can also be coordinated by parents (under your guidance). Preparing concession stands and tickets for concerts, ordering flowers for guest performers, reserving buses and hotels, and photocopying posters and concert programs are all jobs that the parent committee can take off your hands. You will want to oversee the committee so that individual jobs meet with your approval and the program remains your program, but many time-consuming yet crucial duties can largely be taken on by your parent group.

Parent committees not only help you run your program efficiently, they also provide a natural coalition for music education advocacy. If budget cuts threaten your program, you are much better off having these stakeholders already united as a group, rather than attempting to rally support at crunch time. Plus, in times of need, your parent committee can rally additional support throughout the wider parent community, and a strong body of supportive parents carries much more weight with the school and school board officials than any individual teacher. Note: When working with parents, it is important to always keep in mind that you are working together for the benefit of their children. It is essential to develop a relationship of mutual respect with your students' parents and to avoid overburdening them with too many expectations and responsibilities. Your parent group should feel appreciated, not taken for granted.

Parent Communication

One of the simplest strategies for building allies is to be open and friendly with your students' parents. Say hello when you pass them in the hallway or at the grocery store. Stop and have a brief chat about how their child is doing in your class, plans for the upcoming tour, or perhaps simply about the weather. The point is that the more comfortable parents are with you as an individual, the more supportive they will be of you as a teacher. And support for you often translates into support for your program.

Having the occasional friendly word with parents also has the advantage of giving you more information about your students. The fact that they are struggling in English and spending hours with a tutor each night; that they are highly involved in ballet, football, or hockey; that their father is seriously ill—these are important pieces of information to have. They help you to better understand your students and the various life situations that may be affecting their ability to practice, focus, or perform at their best in your class.

Talking with parents in informal settings can give you a sense for whether or not students are practicing at home, as well as provide clues regarding the value attributed to music education by both students and parents. These occasions are valuable opportunities in which to suggest private lessons, extra practice, summer music camp, elite ensemble auditions, better instrument purchases, improved focus and preparation for rehearsals, and any number of other topics you might not necessarily find time in your limited number of spare moments to phone home about.

That being said, there will be occasions when you do need to contact parents in a more formal way—often regarding their child's performance or behavior in class. While such conversations can be stressful, there are steps that you can take to make them as positive and effective as possible. First, it is important to stress the behavior that needs to be addressed, not the student. Parents need to feel that you support their child, that you like and believe in him or her, and that you are a fair teacher. Noting the students' potential, talent, or skill is important in such conversations—in fact, it is usually best to start with the positive before moving into the less positive. Maintaining a log of specific situations that you wish to discuss will help you recall important details when faced with a potentially uncomfortable discussion and can help you maintain objectivity. Sometimes a face-to-face meeting is preferable to a phone conversation, and in difficult situations you might consider inviting the department head or an administrator to sit in on the conversation.

In maintaining professionalism in your relationship with parents it is very important to communicate in a timely manner. A self-imposed twenty-four-hour rule for contacting parents after an incident and for returning parent phone calls and e-mails is an excellent policy. It ensures that situations are dealt with before they have become bigger than they need to be or before the details are lost. It also gives you the appearance of a teacher who is reliable and respectful toward both students and parents. Finally, such a policy allows you to keep on top of your program without having tasks build up unnecessarily.

Communication with parents is an important way of facilitating many matters for your students and assisting them as they grow as musicians and as individuals. It helps gain parents' trust and support for what you are doing as a music educator and, over time, builds a positive, comfortable relationship between you and the parent body—a very influential group within your school community.

Parent-Musicians

Regardless of your school's size, it is very likely that there are musicians among your parent body—moms and dads who play the guitar or piano, played the violin or French horn when they were in school, and sang or continue to sing in community or church choirs. There are also those who are musicians by profession, including those in popular bands, symphony orchestras, and professional or semi-professional choirs; who teach music at a school, conservatory, college, or university; who accompany or perform as session musicians; and those with independent studios. Musicians' children go to school, too, and it is quite possible that some are at yours.

Ask around among your colleagues, administrators, and parents to uncover these peers. You may be surprised at the hidden allies you have.

Find ways to include parent-musicians in your program—chances are good that they will be happy to help build a high-quality music program for their children. Some possible ways they might contribute include accompanying the choir or musical, working with pop bands, giving clinics on specific instruments or voice types, composing, singing, providing contacts within the local music community, and performing at fund-raising events. They may be able to recommend clinicians and performers for special events like Arts Week or even be willing to perform for students themselves. They can also help you to find new teachers for a school-based conservatory program.

In addition to all the valuable, tangible areas in which parent-musicians can help you, they are also natural allies and advocates of music education. Be sure to get to know them and bring them onside with your initiatives. They can add immensely to your strong base of community support.

Parent/Teacher Ensembles

What better way to get parents and teachers to support your program than to actually involve them in it? Among your parent body there are people who played in their high school band or orchestra and who sang in their high school choir. Chances are also good that a few amateur musicians can be found among your fellow teachers. Why not start a band, orchestra, or choir just for the grown-ups? It will give them a chance to tap into their musical selves once again, and to socialize with people they may not otherwise meet. It will also let them get to know you both as a teacher and as a peer.

On the other hand, if you prefer to include the students, you might think about having an ensemble that is specifically a parent/student group. This option has the added benefit of letting parents see you at work with their children, as well as encouraging parents and children to work together for a common purpose. If parents have a personal stake in the music department, you can bet they will stand up for it in times of crisis.

Parents' Day

There's probably no better way of teaching parents what music education is all about than to let them see for themselves. A couple of times each year invite parents to drop by to sit in on your classes, or arrange an open-rehearsal Saturday (a better option for working parents) where families and administrators can witness music education in action. You might ask them to participate in some aspects of the class or to simply observe. Make sure your room is neat and organized, and, if possible, arrange for some coffee and treats for parents to enjoy while there.

Seeing you in action will allow the parents to better appreciate the complexities of your job and of music education in general. By observing the children within their learning environment they will gain a greater understanding of the curriculum and the work that students need to do at home.

Holding a parents' day a couple of times a year is not a big time commitment—for minimal effort and time, you can greatly improve parents' awareness of music education. Very often they are amazed to discover the complex skills that their children are developing in music class. And greater understanding usually translates into increased support.

Parent Support

Let parents know the needs of the department. If you are hoping to raise $10,000 to cover the cost of new choral risers, low brass instruments, an Orff instrumentarium, or recording equipment, make it public knowledge. Not only are people more likely to buy your chocolate bars if they know what the money is for, but you just never know what connections might exist among your school community.

Remember that students have parents, aunts and uncles, and grandparents who all have friends and business associates. It could be that you indirectly have connections to people in music businesses that would be happy to make you a good deal or a donation. Maybe you have connections to a fabric store or seamstress who would love to help make the music uniforms or costumes. Perhaps you have access to a great performance hall in which to present your school concerts for free or at cost. Or maybe a parent works for a top legal firm or is involved in a philanthropic society that would be pleased to make a donation to your program.

You may never know what help is out there unless you let your needs be known—in a newsletter, announcement at a concert or concert program, or through the PTA. A simple statement as to the amount needed, what it is for, and how it will enhance the school, along with an invitation for suggestions and support should suffice in getting the word out to those in a position to help.

IN THE COMMUNITY

Seasoned Teachers

Most teacher training programs require students to spend some time in a school observing and learning from seasoned professionals. It is during this time that student teachers form many of their ideas about the kind of teacher that they would like to be and the kind of program that they would like to have. Additionally, repertoire possibilities and instructional strategies are developed and perspectives are formed about student-teacher interactions. This real-life learning situation helps student teachers develop into independent teachers. While professional teachers may take courses and attend professional workshops and conferences, most do not take further advantage of this unique type of education once they leave the university setting.

Observations do not have to stop once you graduate from college. Most strong teachers would welcome a colleague into their room for a class, a morning, or a full day, as an opportunity to share ideas and learn from each other. You can learn a lot from watching what other people in your field do—some things you'll want to incorporate into your own teaching, and some things you'll want to avoid. You may observe strategies that work better than what you are presently doing; you may also find areas in which your own approach is more successful.

Most schools have a budget for professional development, with a certain amount allocated for each teacher. If you would like to observe a teacher in another school, you may be able to use some of these funds to pay for a substitute teacher for that day. Alternatively, you may be able to schedule the observation on a day when students are away on a field trip or writing exams.

Of course, you don't need to leave your own school to have valuable observation experiences. A lot can be learned from observing how other teachers within your school, including nonmusic teachers, organize their class time, engage student interest, encourage class cooperation, and apply classroom management strategies. It may be equally valuable to observe your students' behavior in other classes. How do they work in other settings and with other teachers? You may find that you can learn a lot about teaching music and about your students when music is taken out of the equation.

As a final note about seasoned teachers, you may want to inquire about mentoring programs within your school or district. Such programs are becoming more and more common, whereby a new teacher is paired with an experienced one who can guide them through some of the challenges of a new teaching career. It can be very reassuring for young teachers to discuss issues and ideas with someone who has been in their shoes and has thrived through many years beyond the first.

Neighboring Schools

Schools that are small or moderately sized, or those that are single-sexed, sometimes find it challenging to fill elite ensembles like stage bands and chamber choirs. They can also have trouble successfully producing high-quality musicals, simply due to a small or select body of students.

If this is the case at your school, one way of offering additional challenging opportunities for your students is to collaborate with neighboring schools. Not only will such collaboration increase the pool of students from which to choose, it will also provide you with additional support to implement your program, effectively halving your work and doubling the number of potential students.

Another option is to offer chamber choir at your school and stage band at the other, or to conjointly offer advanced theory and history courses for which there might not be enough interest in a single school. This way, students at both schools have as many options as possible, but neither your workload nor your colleague's will increase. Collaborating may also give you an opportunity to use resources that are unique to the other school, such as a sound recording studio or an auditorium. Provided that music teachers at both schools are collegial and motivated, collaboration between the two schools can prove beneficial in raising the overall quality of music education throughout the region.

Feeder Schools

Whether you teach elementary, middle, or high school, you will want to establish effective working relationships with schools that are linked to yours. Elementary schools feed into middle schools, middle schools feed into high schools. By working together, music teachers across the school grades can achieve a stronger, more seamless music program for their students. Elementary teachers will want to ensure that their students are properly prepared to enter the middle school program, with all the skills and knowledge that will be expected of them in sixth grade. Middle school teachers will want to encourage as many senior elementary students as possible to continue their music studies once they change schools. The same relationships are true of middle and high school teachers.

It is important for teachers to share their curriculum with their music colleagues in feeder schools and the schools into which they feed. By doing so, everyone will be aware of the levels of student achievement and experience at each educational stage. Teachers must be flexible and willing to make adjustments to their own curriculum, as well as to suggest changes at subsequent and previous levels, that will help to make a smoother overall curriculum for students.

It is also helpful for teachers to sit in on some classes or rehearsals in their "linked" schools to get a better sense of how the curriculum is being implemented and the overall skill level of the students at the previous or subsequent level. Certainly, it is essential for senior students in elementary and middle schools to see and hear students at the next stage perform. Some teachers like to bring representative groups from middle or high schools to perform and answer questions for students at the lower levels. Others find it helpful to bring the younger students on a "tour" of the higher level music department. This latter approach can be particularly effective in giving younger students a fuller picture of the various course options in music.

If the feeder program is large, it may not be feasible to have students visit or sit in on classes, but a demonstration period during which they can sample each of the available options may work well. Actually seeing and hearing the more advanced program can be much more effective in sparking potential students' interest than having them simply read a course title or description.

Local Colleges and Universities

If there is a college or university in your town, why not extend an invitation to its music education students to gain some teaching experience at your school? Enthusiastic, dedicated, and skilled young musicians who are still young enough to be "cool" in your students' eyes can provide excellent role models. They can help to improve your students' skills and open their eyes to the possibility of a career in music—all while freeing up a little of your time to take care of other aspects of your program (be sure to check on school policies regarding inviting visitors to the classroom). Moreover, making positive affiliations with the university builds a positive image for your school. By providing opportunities for preservice teachers you'll also build connections between you and the young people who, in a few short years, will be your colleagues.

Specialists

Very few music teachers feel completely competent with their skills in all aspects of their program. For instance, you might be a super band teacher whose skills on the timpani are less than stellar. Perhaps you are a wonderful choral director but you have never quite felt comfortable dealing with boys' changing voices. Maybe you have lots of young string players at your school for whom you would love to build a string orchestra, but your one-semester string methods course has left you feeling less than confident about the prospect of teaching developing string players.

There is no shame in admitting you're not an expert at everything. You can easily improve your skills and comfort level through consultation with specialists. You undoubtedly have friends, former classmates, or colleagues at other schools who possess the skills you are lacking—get together over lunch or coffee to discuss your needs and ask for their advice.

If your professional development budget allows for it, you might consider going for a lesson or two with an expert or inviting an expert to your school to work with you and your students. If your school can afford it, either through your budget, fund-raising, or user fees, you might hire an expert to work with you and your string group or junior high boys on a regular basis or for a limited period of time. You might even think about taking a course or two at your local university. There are many ways to help raise and continue to hone your skills once you graduate from college. And raising your skill level ultimately is reflected in the success of your students and the overall strength of your program.

Musician Friends

Hearing live performances by expert musicians may be one of the best ways to inspire your students. And, while you will want to bring your students to venues outside the school from time to time, this is not the only way to provide live experiences—you can also bring the musicians to school. And just because you do not have the funds to pay guest performers does not necessarily mean you can not have them.

Musicians know musicians. We all have friends with whom we have studied or played who perform at a very high level. Perhaps they now play professionally in an orchestra or band or as freelance musicians; perhaps they teach music in another school or independently. Invite these professionals to play for your students. They do not necessarily have to perform for the whole school—although this can work very well—but perhaps for a particular class or a select group of students. They might play a recital or perhaps demonstrate some concepts in a few short pieces or excerpts.

It can be very beneficial for your students to hear high-level playing and to interact with other professional musicians besides you. You may want to take your friend to lunch in appreciation of the favor (or possibly reciprocate with a guest appearance at his or her school), and you might be able to offer an honorarium as a token of your thanks (check with the principal about this). The benefits that come from providing excellent live models for your students are invaluable to their growth and the overall success of your program.

Music Teacher Associations

Most provinces and states have organizations whose specific purpose is to unite teachers and support and promote music education throughout the region. Many, like the Canadian Music Educators' Association/ L'Association canadienne des musiciens éducateurs, and MENC: The

National Association for Music Education, have student chapters that you can join for a small fee while still in college. Becoming a member of such organizations is key to making connections with colleagues throughout your region.

During college, classmates often form a support system of like-minded peers who you can learn from and share ideas and concerns with. Some of these classmates may later become colleagues in schools near yours, but many will eventually move on to schools in other parts of the country and world. Since music teachers are often in the position of being the sole music educator in a school, or even across several schools, it is easy for them to feel isolated. It is, therefore, crucial to develop positive relationships with other music educators in your area.

Through conferences, clinics, festivals, and meetings, music teacher associations encourage members to work together, learn from each other, and share their students' achievements. Most music teachers' associations also produce newsletters and sometimes journals that keep members up-to-date on various issues that are important to the profession. Music teacher associations support individual teacher growth, program growth, and the overall goals and quality of music education throughout the region. Advocacy is almost always a priority—within the community and, sometimes, at the government level where budget and subject priority decisions are made that can literally make or break music education programs.

Former Students

Keep informed about what your students are doing once they graduate. Find out if any chose to go into music professionally, either through university programs or through the music industry. If so, get in touch with these individuals and invite them to return to the school to share their experiences with their successors.

It can be very motivating for current students to see those who came before them making a career out of their musical training. You might even invite them to perform at the next school concert, either within an ensemble or as guest soloists. Not only would this be motivating for your students, it would also be a great way of promoting the success of your program with parents, teachers, and administrators.

As a final thought, you may want to ask these former students to join in the making of a school CD. It will add to the excitement for current students and it will raise the profile, quality, and marketability of the final result.

Celebrity Musicians

Send a letter describing your school community and your music program to a music celebrity who is well regarded by your students. Invite him or her to pay a visit—to see your students in action and to talk with them about their own music training (it is best to do a little research and invite those who have had positive training experiences during their school years).

While most people would assume that such a letter would never even be read, a well-worded note to a famous musician might have greater success than you think. Besides, it never hurts to ask. If the celebrity is local, close to local, or will be performing locally, your chances are that much better. Being seen as someone who supports school programs has yet to hurt a celebrity's image.

Other Celebrities

Occasionally you hear of famous actors, athletes, or politicians who grew up playing an instrument in their school band, starring in school musicals, or actually majoring in music at their university. It's a good idea to post photos, articles, biographies, and advertisements of such individuals for students, staff, and parents to see. Write to them, extending an invitation to visit your school and talk with your students about how participation in music enriched their lives.

If they do not live in your area and will not be traveling there in the foreseeable future, why not ask them to send a letter to your students that you can read, discuss, and post? Better yet, set up an opportunity for the students to talk with them online about their experience as a music student. Whether warranted or not, celebrities tend to carry a lot of influence with the general public. Having someone in the public eye endorse what you and your students are doing can build good public relations and a positive image for music in your school.

Local Representatives

If you want support for your music program, you need to let people know about it. Send your minister of education, school board superintendent, or other government representatives an invitation to your next concert, musical, or Battle of the Bands. Although this simple gesture will take but minutes of your time, it can reap long-lasting benefits for your music department. These are the people who can work for or against music education. And unless they are musicians themselves or have children involved in music programs, they may find it difficult to support an area of study they know little about.

If you think it is pointless to send an invitation, that it will be ignored, think again. Politicians make their living on maintaining an appearance of being "one of the people", and more often than not, they will turn up when invited. Ask them to RSVP so that you can be sure to reserve a seat of honor. Also, be sure to recognize their presence from the podium. You might even ask them to say a few words to the audience.

A visit from your political leaders can help you on many levels. It educates the powers that be about music education, which can help build support for your program and others in the region. Hosting invited dignitaries makes the school look good for attracting the attention of a community leader and validates your program with parents. Such visits make the principal look good for building programs that attract high-profile attention, and make you look good—with the principal for thinking to invite the guest and with the students, parents, and teachers for building a program that would make such a person want to attend. Generally, it is a winning situation that takes such minimal effort.

Music Industry Representatives

If you live in or near a big city, there are likely to be industry people nearby. Why not set up a visit for people in the business to talk with your students about what they do and what it takes to be discovered. How do you make a demo? Find gigs? Get noticed? Get signed? Whether or not you have any students with the ability or desire to go into the music business, there will be a keen interest in knowing more about the inner workings of it.

This type of presentation will gain the interest of both students and teachers and will seem a progressive move for a music department, where too often the reputation tends to be anything but progressive. Such an event would not take very much organization or time on your part (get your parents' committee involved). It could, however, contribute significantly to interest in your program.

FINANCIAL FRIENDS

Patrons

Whether in schools or in the wider community, arts programs tend to be cash-strapped. Because of this, fund-raising can take an increasing amount of a music teacher's time. Remember, however, that it is the school district's responsibility to fully fund the music program. One low-effort approach to raising funds is through advertising for music suppliers in exchange for their financial support of your program.

Ask for a special rate on scores, uniforms, instruments, equipment, supplies, or piano tuning. In exchange for a good rate, you can offer to put a promotional advertisement or note of thanks on your school concert program. Good business people will see this as a great opportunity

for endorsement, since the people who will read your concert program—
parents of school-age children—compose the very demographic toward
which they gear much of their business.

Parents purchase instruments, supplies, and music for their children
and they get their pianos tuned (when reminded). Having an advertisement on the back of the school concert program is a great way for music
businesses to stay in the forefront of parents' minds when it comes to purchasing supplies and services—it may even get the ball rolling toward the
purchase of their child's first flute or the annual piano tuning. And parents will be happy to support businesses that support their school. Making good business arrangements with local music suppliers can be mutually beneficial, saving money for you and making money for them.

Donations

If you would like to provide some extras for your program, you might
try acquiring some assets from the community. For example, if you'd like
to keep some spare guitars at school for students who forget theirs at
home or to assist a student who may not be able to afford even an inex-
pensive instrument rental, you might appeal to parents or to wider community.

Many households have long-forgotten instruments in their basements
and attics—instruments that someone, sometime, long ago played, but
that have since been collecting dust. You may be able to round up enough
decent instruments to keep spares in your classroom or to help out students without financial resources. Do be sure to check on any school policies regarding donations before you make your appeal. You should also
inquire as to whether or not tax receipts might be made available for
donors.

Once you've gotten the go-ahead from your principal you might even
take the appeal one step further and send out notices to local businesses,
churches, and community organizations such as the Lions Club, Rotary
Club, or the Knights of Columbus, who are often happy to support a good
cause. Members of your parent committee could help organize the search
and arrange to pick up donated instruments. With a little initiative you
may have your spare instruments sooner than you think—with almost no
outlay of cash.

Music Businesses

It is important to foster a good relationship with your local music store.
By doing so, you will be opening the door to possibilities for your pro-

gram. I know one teacher at an underprivileged school who regularly negotiates significantly lower prices on her choral scores and elementary musicals by dealing exclusively with a single store and building up a relationship with the owners. Often music stores that sell or rent instruments are eager to provide instrument demonstrations and trials at schools for students in the process of selecting one to learn—provided that you allow them to make a pitch for their rental program with parents.

As well, you may be able to garner fund-raising support from your music store. I have heard of a piano dealer willing to sell a piano at below cost to a school music department for the purpose of fund-raising (as a silent auction item). When purchasing new instruments a number of years ago I did not have enough funds to buy a new teacher saxophone. However, because I had given a lot of business to the particular store, they threw the saxophone in "on loan" for as long as we needed it. Even if a music store lets you leave your fund-raising chocolate bars on the counter for customers to purchase, this can result in increased money for program extras. Remember that the music business is a two-way street—if you bring business their way, music dealers can help you out a lot.

If you live in a smaller area that has only one or two music stores, you might consider a diplomatic approach by dealing with each store for particular items, so that the wealth and good will is spread throughout your community. You will want to avoid appearing as though you are playing the businesses off one another. Especially in areas where there are fewer businesses, but also in larger communities, you may want to discuss the matter with your principal before making any agreements toward exclusivity. He or she may have concerns about appearing to favor one business over another, or there may be historical issues or agreements with certain distributors that you should know about. Your efforts toward spending the school's funds most effectively will be noted and you may avoid any unnecessary complications that could arise.

SUMMARY

In order to build strong, respected music programs, effective teachers need to foster positive relationships with a variety of individuals and groups within and outside the school walls. Colleagues, parents, other teachers, music merchants, music faculties, former students, and other members of the community each have special contributions they can make to the development of a school music program. The job of the music teacher is to understand the role that these people can play and to reach out to them for assistance and support—to build a solid network of advocates and assistants.

ASSIGNMENTS

1. Poll the teachers at a local school regarding their participation in music while in elementary, high school, college, and as an adult. What percentage of the nonarts teachers were involved in music during each time period? What did this involvement entail—instrumental or choral ensembles, private instruction, musical theatre, rock bands, church choir . . . ? How has participation in music been a positive force in their lives?

2. Make a list of the strengths and weaknesses you perceive in yourself as a future music teacher. For the items on your weakness list, plan realistic ways to strengthen them and provide strong learning experiences for your students in these areas.

3. Develop a list of contacts—people you can turn to for advice, support, and clinics. Who could you ask for low brass or jazz band support? Choreography? Repertoire ideas? Categorize your list and maintain it as you start your career and make new contacts at festivals, meetings, workshops, and through colleagues.

4. Develop a strategy for starting up a parent-teacher-student ensemble. What type of ensemble will it be? Will prior training be required? If so, what will the criteria be? What recruitment strategies will you use? How will repertoire be selected?

5. Research local public figures or musical celebrities, local or otherwise, with respect to their participation in music education. Compose a letter that you might send inviting them to visit your school to speak with your students about their experiences and the value that music education has made in their lives. Save this letter for future use.

6. Plan your first parent committee meeting. How will it be structured? Write a letter inviting parents to attend the meeting and join the committee. What will you tell them about yourself, your plans for the program, and the expectations of committee members? Create a sign-up list and include jobs that parents can choose from. Will a parent-leader be chosen? If so, how? What other administrative positions will be required?

7. Research the local music industry. What types of resources are available in the area/region in which you plan to work? How could these be used to support your program?

8. Examine your provincial or state curriculum guide for one or more subject areas outside music at either the elementary, middle, or high school level. For each grade within that school level, make a list of connections that can be made between that subject and music. How can these connections be used to draw support for your program?

9. Write a letter to a real or fictitious community leader describing your program—its role and importance within your school. Invite him or her to be a guest of honor at an upcoming performance. Save this letter for future use.

10. Visit a local music store and speak with the owner/manager about his or her support of school music programs. Do they provide school discounts? Will they help with fund-raising efforts? Do they provide special rates for student rentals? Will they provide instrument demonstrations and tryouts for beginning students? Are there other ways they can support your program?

Chapter 3

Students

The overriding key to success in any music program lies in the students. Students who are excited about music and truly engaged in music learning and performing are the lifeblood of music education. One of our primary goals as music educators, then, is to create a learning environment that is rich in opportunities for student success and engagement with music. Students who are dedicated to their school music program are the best advocates for music education in their school, homes, and wider community—today as students, and in a few short years as parents, teachers, administrators, and policy makers.

This chapter focuses on creating opportunities to build student skills in ways that are nurturing and exciting, providing students with the necessary tools to maintain lifelong music learning and enjoyment. Included are ideas for making music classes joyous, memorable events; suggestions for recognizing student achievement; and strategies for making music education as accessible as possible for all students.

LEADERSHIP

Student Music Committee

Students today are involved in many aspects of school life. There are music ensembles, athletic teams, extracurricular clubs, organizing committees, and student council. One way to tap into students' dedication to the music department is to help them create a Music Students' Committee. This group can support you and the overall program in a variety of ways, leaving many jobs for you to oversee and approve, rather than physically implement. Some potential tasks that students can take on include organizing scores, administering the music listening program (see "Music to Start the Day," at the end of this chapter), announcing achievements in music, setting up audience chairs for concerts, taking photos at music events, getting notices out to students, and maintaining a neat room and bulletin board—just to name a few.

Belonging to a Music Committee gives students a sense of responsibility and eases your workload. Perhaps most importantly, it gives students a sense of ownership in the department, which builds dedicated and vocal advocates for it. It is important, however, not to overburden your committee or to monopolize its time. As mentioned earlier, student life can be a busy one, with many people and activities vying for time. You will want to keep an eye open for students who are spending all their time "hanging out" in the music room to the exclusion of other aspects of school life. The goal is to develop a sense of community, pride, and ownership in the music department, but also to help students develop as well-rounded individuals.

Section Leaders

Looking for ways to increase student practice time without increasing your already packed schedule? Try designating some ensemble responsibilities to section leaders. Not only will it achieve the above goal, it will also build leadership skills in your section leaders and tighter ensemble skills within the individual members.

When setting up your sectional program, it is important to emphasize the value of the rehearsals in improving individual playing and overall quality and cohesion of each section. Working with your students' schedules, arrange for regular meeting times for each section. Lunchtime often works well—just be sure to give students enough time to actually eat, too.

Prepare an outline of material that needs to be worked on at each rehearsal and, if necessary, meet briefly with section leaders to discuss specific components. On the rehearsal form, provide a space for section leaders to indicate which components they worked on and which they did not have time for, as well as problems they encountered, students who were uncooperative, and absences.

Depending on the rules of your school you may need to be present while students are rehearsing in sections. Even so, letting the section leaders run the rehearsal frees you up to work on other things while still being present in the room. In addition to running sectional rehearsals, section leaders can also take on the responsibility of managing scores for their section, handing out parts and ensuring that they are returned.

You may want to change section leaders every term so as to reward dedication and effort and to provide opportunities for other students in the ensemble to rise to the position. Developing leadership and group skills in your music students can help them hone their teaching and learning skills, allow them to take ownership of the ensemble, and raise the ensemble's overall group cohesion and musicianship.

Student Demonstrations

Older students are important role models in their schools. Younger students look up to them, taking their cues about what is socially acceptable. Asking students in the upper grades to provide demonstrations of various musical skills can be a great strategy in getting younger students excited and eager to learn.

Tapping into this resource within your own program can benefit students at both ends. The older students have the opportunity to serve as "experts" and gain valuable leadership experience. This contributes to their self-esteem and their sense of pride in their musical achievements. The younger students not only have the opportunity to learn from their older counterparts, but also gain a sense of the growth and continuity of musical skills throughout the school grades—in a sense giving them a taste of the bigger picture of music education in their school.

Visits to Other Classes

Instead of having older students provide demonstrations for younger classes (as mentioned in the previous paragraph), a related strategy is to provide opportunities for younger students to observe or work with older grades. Let them hear the repertoire the older students are playing; let them see you interacting with the higher grades. Such occasions give younger students opportunities to hear higher-level playing throughout the year (not just at the concert), to get a feel for the various instruments and voice types, as well as the skills and techniques they should be working toward, and to get excited about the musical opportunities your program offers at the higher grades.

Observations allow younger students to see and hear a level to strive toward, and build a sense of anticipation for higher-level achievement. There are benefits for the older students as well—additional opportunities to perform and to be leaders, teachers, and role models. Each occasion where more and less advanced students come together to learn from each other helps build an overall cohesion and sense of community across grades within the music department.

Music Scholarships

High schools award scholarships for academic achievement. Many also recognize areas such as athletics and citizenship. It is important to also have one or more awards for music. If your school doesn't already have one on the books, you might consider working toward this addition to the award roster. A scholarship for music recognizes musical excellence as a skill requiring dedication and hard work, as something challenging to attain and an achievement on par with other school subjects. It gives students something to strive for and take pride in, as well as to help finance continued music study.

To begin a scholarship fund, get your parent committee involved in organizing a special fund-raiser specifically for this purpose. Perhaps a concert or cabaret night with performances by seniors might be a suitable start. Your parents' committee may well be able to secure a donation from a member of the community who would like a scholarship in music made in his or her name or that of a loved one. However you come up with the funds, getting the ball rolling toward a music scholarship fund is a worthwhile venture to undertake.

Leadership and Achievement

Varsity teams have colors, jackets, and jerseys to denote their membership in an important school team. Captains, in particular, are specially marked as leaders in the school. You can take a cue from the varsity coaches and recognize those within your ensembles and classes who have shown particular leadership and dedication. Specially made school music pins are one example of an effective way to denote leadership in the music department. They can be custom-made in a bulk order that will last for years at minimal expense to the department. A certificate with the pin provides a permanent record of the achievement.

Another way to recognize achievement and dedication to the school music program is to create an honor society, such as a chapter of MENC's Tri-M Music Honor Society. Admission to such a group is an excellent way to show students that their hard work and valuable contribution to the department is noted and valued, which can be a wonderful motivator for those inducted into the group, as well as for those who aspire to do so. As an added bonus, an honor society crosses all areas of the music department, so leaders in individual ensembles or classes are brought together as a united musical-excellence team, which can provide a major boost to your department. Tri-M chapters can begin as early as sixth grade and provide students with additional music opportunities within the community and across the country.

Ask your school principal to include any music awards at the formal awards ceremony for all subject areas. This sets up a mindset in which music is on par with other school departments. It recognizes those who have worked hard in building their own and their classmates' skills and musicianship, and provides a tangible reward toward which other students can strive. Awards ceremonies are also good opportunities to recognize other achievements in music that students have made. Successes in competition, membership in music societies, other awards and scholarships in music are all achievements that should be publicly noted and lauded at school.

The Gifted and Talented

Every music teacher comes upon the occasional student who shows great promise as a musician and/or demonstrates advanced skills for his or her age. These are the potential music teachers, performers, and music industry professionals of the future. We are privileged to count them among our students.

Gifted and talented students can also provide special challenges for the music teacher. With large class sizes and the identification of more and more students with special learning needs, teachers in most subject areas often have difficulty taking care of the needs of those whose skills and abilities exceed those of the average student. Group performance classes such as band, orchestra, and choir can prove to be particularly challenging in this regard, since it is not always easy to provide more challenging material for these individuals.

Music teachers need to be creative in finding appropriate teaching strategies to reach and engage the gifted and talented students in their classes. Discipline problems, boredom, frustration, apathy, and even poor achievement can arise if students have already mastered the material being taught. It is not uncommon for musically talented students to drop out of or refuse to take part in the school music program. While gifted and talented students can easily, often effortlessly, manage the regular class material, they should never be overlooked as not needing extra support or attention. Their needs may simply be at a higher level than those of their same-age peers.

Strategies for challenging high-achieving students can be as unique as the students themselves. Some ideas include having additional performances to work toward, more comprehensive study of a particular style such as blues or jazz, composing, conducting or arranging music, studying higher-level repertoire, advanced music theory and history lessons, study of a new or related instrument, and joining an ensemble or class usually reserved for older students.

This last option may require some effort with respect to convincing administrators, teachers, and parents, because pulling the student from other classes to attend rehearsals might be required. (In successful pull-out programs, there are usually very strict rules about completing work missed from other subjects while attending rehearsals.) If it can be arranged, the extra musical challenge for talented students can be very rewarding.

Providing leadership roles such as assisting new or lower-achieving students can also be an effective teaching and learning strategy for both the gifted student and the person they are assisting. Caution needs to be taken, however, in this area. While teaching another person can be an excellent way to hone one's own skills, not everyone has the temperament or desire to teach. Consistently employing gifted students in this manner may work well for some and poorly for others—teachers need to use their own judgment when implementing this strategy. It is also important to not simply use these students as additional arms, so to speak. They have a right to be taught and to learn at their own level, so while assisting others is an approach that can be used occasionally, it should not be the only way that teachers engage their talented students.

Students Requiring Additional Support

In most music programs there are also some students who require additional support to achieve at grade level. This may include students who are new to the school who have not had similar, or perhaps any, musical training, students who decide to join an instrumental program in secondary school without training in the earlier grades, students with learning disabilities, students who became excited about music after the school musical but do not have any theoretical background—students who, for one reason or another, are not quite at the same level as their peers.

This situation can be very challenging for the music teacher, who typically has far too many things on his or her plate. Before and after school, recess, and lunchtimes are often used to schedule sectionals, rehearsals, auditions, and playing tests. So, how do you find ways to support those who need help, while still maintaining your planned curriculum and rehearsals?

Creative teachers find many positive ways to help students either catch up to their classmates or to work with them effectively at their own skill level. Some involve peers in the learning process—as peer tutors outside class time or as partners during class time. When pairing students together, it is important to look not only at the achievement level of the students providing support, but also their social skills, positive attitude, and natural teaching abilities. Pairing a struggling student with a gifted student who is impatient and has difficulty understanding why others don't "get" the material in the same way he or she does could leave the student being "helped" in an even more vulnerable position.

If you can find time in your schedule to provide individual or small-group instruction to students who need it, this can work very well—provided that the students can be available when you are. This is often the sticking point. Unless you have time when students are not in classes—before or after school, at recess or lunchtime (and even then the students may not be available or able to arrive early/leave late)—there is the matter of arranging for them to be with you when they are supposed to be in another class.

Some schools will not allow students to be pulled out for music programs. Others have very successful pull-out programs for their entire instrumental program. Some parents will not permit their child to miss one subject's class to improve another area. If this is an option you would like to consider, you will need to clear it with all parties—the principal, students, parents, and teachers—before making a decision to proceed. If it is not a permanent arrangement, but rather a limited number of extra tutorials, you may have more luck in gaining support.

It may be feasible, in some schools, for students to take private instruction that will help them catch up to the level of their classmates more quickly. This will depend largely on the financial situation of your school community, in addition to the interest and support for the student's music education on the part of his or her parents. If your budget will support it, you may be able to help finance a limited number of lessons or some small-group instruction by an independent instructor.

Aside from pairing students with a classmate, what other steps can you take in class to support students? For ensemble classes, you can put your arranging skills to work. Arrange scores so that parts are more accessible for students with new or slowly developing skills. This will allow them to work effectively with their same-age peers, but with a more manageable part. In other classes, adapt lessons so as to provide for participation by students with more and less advanced skills and avoid putting students with weaker skills in a competitive or potentially embarrassing situation. For instance, in elementary classes you should avoid having students individually read notated pitches or rhythms (such as rhythm-relay type games) if there are students who cannot yet do this successfully.

One final suggestion is to incorporate computer-assisted instruction into your teaching. There are so many wonderful software programs available for music education that are both educational and motivational. Put this technology to use in your class and ensemble rooms to focus on developing the skills that individual students may be lagging behind in.

MAKING IT MEMORABLE

Student Field Trips

School field trips are among the most memorable occasions of school days. They allow students to experience life beyond the walls of the school and add to their knowledge and skill, all while having a good time. Consider taking your students on a performing tour. It can be a simple weekend trip to towns close by, singing or playing at churches or community halls or collaborating with other ensembles. Or it can be a bigger endeavor, taking students farther from home to a different province or state, even a different country. If your performing groups are particularly strong, you might think about entering competitions on a national or international level.

The band, orchestra, or choir trip can be a major enticement for students to continue participating in the music program from year to year and provides a tangible goal to work toward. Of course, trips can also be an enormous amount of work for the teacher, so recruitment of parents and teachers to assist in the planning and organization is a must. Benefits come in the form of motivation for students to improve their playing skills, enticement to continue performing in (or join) an ensemble, social cohesion within the group, opportunities for students to hone their performance skills, and increased status of the music program within the school and beyond.

CDs

Recording your students' music making can be exciting and motivating, as well as profile building. It helps to focus students' efforts on high-quality performance and validates their achievements on a very tangible level. With a recording goal set from the beginning of the school year, students are encouraged to work hard to ensure that the CD represents their best possible performance.

Recordings help to raise your program's profile with students, parents, and staff, giving it a progressive image. Educationally, the process affords students the opportunity to become familiar with some of the intricacies involved in making a professional music recording. Making a recording can be viewed as an extrinsic reward after a year's hard work and achievement. On a purely practical note, you can make copies of the CD to sell to parents, use it to promote your program in the wider school community, and to send to music competitions, festivals, and conferences.

Recording a CD is a lot of work and a permanent record of where a program is at a given point in time. I would recommend that teachers wait until they have been teaching in a given school for at least a few years before undertaking such a project. In addition to selecting, learning, and polishing the repertoire, it involves planning well in advance of the actual recording sessions, booking sound recording engineers and venues for the recording, raising funds to pay for the recording, working out agreeable times with colleagues and parents as to when students can be freed from other obligations to make the recording, and dealing with publishing companies and/or their agency to arrange for permission and payment of royalties to the publisher and composer.

This last point is of particular importance, since it is one that beginning teachers might not necessarily be aware of. Unless the music being performed is now in the public domain, copyright law dictates that the use of photocopies of sheet music by performing groups is illegal, that permission is required, and that royalties must be paid for any recordings made of the work. There is, of course, a great deal more to copyright law than these three points—much more than the scope of this book provides for. All music teachers would be well advised to take some time to learn what the law covers, as it will inevitably affect their work.

To this end, MENC: the National Association for Music Education has a webpage that answers frequently asked questions about copyright for music educators and provides a number of important links to help in the process at www.menc.org/resources/view/copyright-center.

While copyright law must be respected, don't let the royalty issue deter you from making a recording with your group once you have established yourself and your program in the school. Adhering to it is not nearly as complicated as it may sound, and the above-noted website can guide you through the process with relative ease. Obtaining permission and paying royalties are issues that you can certainly solicit help with from a colleague or member of the parent committee. Keep in mind that the benefits of producing a recording with your students may ultimately significantly outweigh the costs. And, as with most things in life, the first time is always the hardest.

Music Software

Technology permeates almost every aspect of our lives, jobs, and schools today. Children learn to use computers from the outset of their schooling (and often sooner) and become proficient on them early. For music education, there are a number of excellent computer programs designed for developing many skill areas—from ear training and theoretical skills to tuning, composing, and practicing with an ensemble. There are programs that offer tutorials, test students' skills, and challenge them with educational games.

By having such programs available on the school computers (not just in the music rooms, but in the labs as well), students will be encouraged, enticed even, to improve their musical skills. Most programs are very motivating, interactive, and include high-quality graphics, so students often learn in spite of themselves. This addition to the program will be seen as innovative and in touch with modern society—allowing you to appear progressive while ultimately improving individual student skills and overall program quality.

In addition to programs for students, it is essential for the teacher to become familiar with music notation software. Most music teachers plan compositional activities for their students, and preparing examples or helping students use the software requires a basic knowledge of the software. Sometimes composing songs to demonstrate music concepts or to fill gaps in the repertoire is required. At the secondary level, music teachers often spend time arranging parts for missing instrument lines, for boys' changing voices, or to accommodate less advanced students. Keeping in mind copyright laws governing arrangements, simplified editions, transcriptions, and adaptations, notational software allows teachers to make these arrangements more efficiently and effectively—not to mention more neatly. Again, consult the MENC copyright center website (www.menc.org/resources/view/copyright-center) for guidance with arrangements or limit your arranging to songs in the public domain.

At the university level, most music education programs now offer some training in music technology for prospective teachers. Some courses focus primarily on tools for the teacher—typically, notation programs—while others run the gamut of what's available for music education in general. If your background did not include such a course, you might consider looking into what's available. Some colleges offer the technology component as part of a summer program—a great time for teachers to pick up additional courses that they did not take as a student.

Music educator organizations frequently include technology/software clinics in their professional development offerings. These clinics are regularly offered at music educator conferences. At larger conferences, you can often browse the software offerings and get firsthand information about programs and other technology support tools directly from company representatives at the conference marketplace. Websites for music software often contain samplers that you can download to test out and see whether it might fit your students' needs before committing to a purchase. MENC is a good resource—the website, journals, and conferences—for finding information about and suggestions for software purchases.

TI:ME (Technology Institute for Music Educators) is a professional organization that focuses specifically on the development and use of technology in music education. They offer a variety of courses (and a certification program) in many states—primarily in the summer months—that can help you build the skills that you need to effectively incorporate technology into your teaching (see their website for details: www.ti-me.org). These courses cover the full gamut of technology for music educators—in addition to software training, there are also courses that deal with multimedia, using electronic instruments, recording, and others. They are an excellent resource for music educators who want to build their technology skills.

Social Time

When rehearsals are not part of the regular school day, teachers are left with only three real possibilities for scheduling them: (1) early mornings, when students are often fresh and focused, but may have trouble arriving on time; (2) lunchtime, students' only substantial break during the school day, during which some time must necessarily be taken up with eating; (3) after school, when their brains are tired and their bodies are restless.

For various reasons, many teachers must opt for the after-school time. If this is the case in your school, you might consider incorporating some social time into your practice for a more effective and motivating rehearsal. If your choir rehearsal is from 3:30 to 5:00, you might break it up into two sessions—3:30 to 4:10 and 4:20 to 5:00—with a supervised break in between.

Remember that however keen your students may be, they are still kids and they have been at work since 8:00 or 9:00 in the morning. If you feel the need for a break at the end of the school day, then imagine how much more your students must need one. Giving them a break in the middle of a rehearsal allows a little time to have a snack and to socialize with their friends. It also rejuvenates the students, and you, for a more focused second half. So, instead of waning energy, students will come back more energetic than ever.

Rehearsal Parties

School rehearsals are normally held during the school week. Prior to important performances, however, you may find yourself needing a little extra time in which to add the finishing touches. With all your students' other commitments, it can be a challenge inspiring them to come for extra evening or weekend rehearsals. One way to achieve this is to turn the rehearsal into a social event.

Send a notice home that, in preparation for upcoming events, you will be holding a special rehearsal followed by a party to celebrate students' hard work and achievement throughout the year. You might ask each student to contribute a couple of dollars to cover the cost of the food or for parents to send cookies to complete the spread. Perhaps you have a little money designated in your budget or fund-raising account for student get-togethers.

While students may initially complain about having an extra rehearsal, you will likely find that rehearsal parties turn into important bonding experiences. Of all the time your students spend together in rehearsals and performances, they actually have few opportunities to simply hang out and socialize with each other. The combination of rehearsal and party can be beneficial in both the immediate effects of improving current repertoire and in the long-term effects of ensemble cohesion, unity, and support. The more your students identify themselves as part of this group, the greater their pride will be in being affiliated with it, and the more appealing it will seem to those not presently involved.

Weekend Retreats

Elite community ensembles commonly use weekend retreats to jump-start the year. This is a creative approach that gets music learning under way, skills warmed up, and bonds formed among students prior to the beginning of the school year. This model can easily be followed in your school program too.

Make arrangements for the retreat before the end of the school year so that parents can include it when making summer plans. Try to book a venue that can support your full ensemble and also provide a few rooms for students to sleep in. Late August/early September is the ideal time for a retreat, and you may find summer campgrounds available at this time. Alternatively, one of your students may have a summer cottage that is big enough for you to use. Or, if all else fails, you can invite students to bring their sleeping bags to school and hold the event there.

Ball games, outings, campfires, and barbecues all add to the spirit of the weekend (they can't practice *all* the time) and provide valuable opportunities for students to bond. Your rehearsal time can be divided into sectionals in which to learn parts and full rehearsals in which the first of the year's selections start to come together. In the end, your intense practice weekend will result in setting students on course for the year while providing what students remember as a weekend get-away filled with fond memories of their ensemble experience.

As a beginning teacher, you may prefer to wait a few years before undertaking a full weekend retreat, with all the organization, chaperone, and liability issues that it necessarily entails. And be sure to discuss the details and get the go-ahead from your principal before making any plans for overnight events. Retreats can also work well as day-only events—the only difference being that the venue would necessarily need to be local for drop-off and pick-up.

Outside Concerts

Experiencing live orchestras, operas, musicals, big bands, and other musical events and ensembles can be very exciting and educational for your students. It is so important to bring them out into the community, perhaps even on a trip to a larger center, to experience a live professional performance in its traditional setting. No longer will an orchestra be a poster on the wall or a sound from a CD. Instead, it can become a real, tangible ensemble that exists and performs in modern society, an ensemble that people pay to hear perform. The music they perform comes alive, and is not a remnant from another time.

Attending live performances outside the school environment lets students learn and develop appropriate concert behavior. As well, it lets your school be seen in the community as culturally and musically grounded. Most parents support providing a cultural education for their children, even if the events are not something they personally know much about. You might even consider inviting parents to join you on these trips, which can serve to better educate them musically, provide opportunities to build a relationship with you, allow them to participate in high-quality musical experiences with their children, and provide additional supervision for students.

While music field trips are exciting educational ventures, it is not always necessary to take students out to see and hear professional performances. Many professional ensembles have educational outreach programs that bring them directly into the schools. In some cases, the groups will not only perform, but also incorporate students and/or student ensembles into the show or give workshops for relevant classes. Such performances can draw community members into the school—thereby highlighting the music program—as well as allow the students to have closer contact with professional musicians and make better use of the out-of-class time than the typical music field trip in which travel time needs to be incorporated into the overall schedule.

Popular Music

For at least forty years now, a topic of debate among music educators has been whether or not popular music should be included in the school music curriculum. The profession has been slow to accept styles of music outside the traditional classical genre. And while jazz and world music have gained general acceptance in the music classroom, the jury is still out, in many places, on the inclusion of popular music. It seems that every teacher has his or her own opinion about this matter (and certainly this book is not the forum for a philosophical debate). The only point I would like you to consider is this: inundating students with art music to the exclusion of more popular repertoire may not be the key to a successful program.

Most music teachers have been trained to play and teach classical music; they prefer to base their school programs on it, and hope to foster an understanding and respect for art music among their students. However, including some repertoire that is more relevant to your students' experience can be very valuable to your program. It is important to keep in mind that very few children grow up in households where art music is the preferred listening fare; it is not common for parents to take their children to the symphony or opera; and your students do not watch Cecilia Bartoli on MTV. Popular music is the music students know, prefer, and can relate to. It is likely that some of your students dream of, even strive toward, having a career in the popular music industry.

Opting to include the occasional selection of popular music into your program helps bring students from the known to the unknown, which is one of the main aims of music education. There is a wide variety of traditional ensemble arrangements for varying ranges of skills—from beginner to advanced. In general music classes you might consider analyzing the components of a selection of popular music in the same way you would study a selection of art music. After all, we consider the music of many world cultures to be appropriate listening fare—why not treat contemporary popular music with the same respect?

This type of open-mindedness can be a way of connecting with your students. In the teaching of art music, jazz, and world music, you ask students to open their ears and minds to less familiar styles of music and to show a healthy respect for them. By doing the same with popular music, you will set a good example of "practice what you preach" for your students.

The inclusion of popular music can make your program more appealing to a wider array of students. Those with natural musical abilities but no prior training or experience with art music may be much more inclined to join an ensemble that incorporates music they have experience with and understand. This music can often serve as a bridge connecting students to more standard repertoire.

Music Camps

Encourage your students to consider attending a music camp during summer holidays as a fun way of building their skills. Collect brochures and post them on your department bulletin board. Talk to your students about how fun, inspiring, and educational camps can be, and note the fact that they are great places to meet talented and like-minded young people from other schools and towns. Try to dispel any ideas about music camps being boring or "uncool." If you teach at a camp, students may be that much more inclined to sign up. Bring photos of both music and non-music-related activities from a recent camp to give your students a sense of the environment. You might even personally encourage particularly keen or talented students to consider applying. Be sure to let students know about any scholarships or bursaries they may be eligible for.

Not only will their musical skills improve (instead of deteriorate) over the summer months, but your students will return to school with greater confidence and pride in their abilities and affiliation with the music department. Such confidence and pride can be contagious and help to promote group pride within your ensemble. Once a few students have had a positive experience at music camp, you will likely find more attending in subsequent years. Before long, this can result in improved overall skill and musicianship levels in your ensembles.

Your Own Music Camp

As an alternative to sending your students away for camp, consider setting up your own. Schools have many unused rooms in the summer months, making them ideal venues for day camps. Invite local musicians to spend a couple of weeks giving lessons or directing ensembles. Have a beginning jazz band, marching band, show choir, or musical theatre production in which students can get their first taste of these types of ensembles. By setting up a camp on your own school campus, you are likely to attract more of your students than would normally sign up for an outside music camp.

It is a good idea to open the camp to students from other local schools in addition to your own. This way, your students will have a chance to work with and get to know musically oriented students from the wider community, and you can be more confident about having enough students to make the camp a success. Incorporating fun activities such as ball games and barbecues helps to break up the day, gives students' voices and embouchures a break from music making, and provides a lighter side to the camp. When September rolls around, students will be in good shape to start the new school year on a high note. They will require less review than would normally be required after a summer's hiatus, and will bring positive memories and attitudes about music back to their school ensemble.

District Ensembles

Working in elite ensembles can be rewarding for individual high-level students. The additional challenge, repertoire, and rehearsal time will improve your students' skills, which will, in turn, raise the overall skill level of your ensemble. You can post concert and audition information for elite ensembles on your notice board and encourage students to attend them. If one or more of your students are currently in such an ensemble, their classmates may be more interested in attending. Chances are good that they will be impressed, perhaps even motivated to improve their own skills in order to try out at the next round of auditions.

Be sure to post and let students know about upcoming auditions for any ensembles that you think would be appropriate and appealing to them. Advancing their skills and interest, whether in or outside school, will ultimately benefit both the individual students and your school program.

Celebrations

Student successes are not foregone conclusions. As such, it is important that we recognize occasions of achievement. When your choir sings at the hospital, your band or orchestra plays at a festival, and your fourth-graders present their musical play, be sure to conclude with a small celebration. This can be as simple as donuts on the bus ride home.

Of primary importance in each celebration are your words of recognition and praise for their accomplishment. Students need to know that they are valued, that their successes have been acknowledged, and, most especially, that you are proud of them. So have a pizza party, a dessert party, a barbecue-and-baseball party, or simply a homemade cookie party. Just be sure to celebrate achievement and express pride in your students as individuals, as young musicians, and as an ensemble.

BEYOND THE MUSIC ROOM

The Pianists and Guitarists

Every school has students who are involved in music outside the school program. Pianists and guitarists are particularly common and, unlike their counterparts on the violin who are typically involved in string orchestras, these students very often act exclusively as soloists. It is important to integrate these students into your program.

Whether you teach at the elementary or secondary level, you are likely to have at least one student playing at a high enough level on the piano or guitar to be able to accompany vocal ensembles or individuals. Perhaps they might not have the skills or the time to be the regular accompanist, but they can play for the occasional selection. Invite them to perform at assemblies and talent shows or lead the national anthem at concerts.

This strategy brings students who are traditionally soloists into the ensemble scene, incorporating those who may not have been previously involved in the music department (even though they are deeply involved in music). Bringing these students into the fold recognizes their achievements, raises the overall standard of your ensembles, encourages their growth, and sets a model of hard work and dedication for other students.

Individual Competitions

From time to time you will come across notices regarding competitions for students—for compositions, performances, or essays. Be sure to post these notices on your music board and bring them to students' attention in class. Encourage individuals you know to be good contenders to consider participating. You might even design a class assignment that centers about the particular competition.

This type of event can give students something new to strive toward— a reason to put the finishing touches on a work or to consolidate their thoughts on a matter. A win or honorable mention could be the launching pad for a musical career. As well, the public recognition would associate the winning student with your school, in particular with your music department, and reflect a strong, successful program.

Nonmusical Endeavors

While your music commitments undoubtedly keep your schedule jam-packed, it is important to also display an interest in other school events and activities. Go to see the school play, basketball championship, debating final, and science fair. Chaperone a school dance and accompany a nonmusic field trip. Any chance you have to see another side of your students and to let them see another side of you can contribute to a strong student-teacher relationship. As well, students not currently involved in the music program will have a chance to meet and get to know you, which may inspire interest in your classes and ensembles.

As a music teacher, you are a very busy person and will not be able to attend all school events. However, it is important to attend some nonmusic events when possible, if only for a few minutes to drop in and say hello. These efforts will help integrate you with the school community and allow you to know more about your students' interests and skills. It also shows students that you support them as individuals with diverse interests and abilities, not only as musicians. And it shows a respect for and interest in the work of your fellow teachers—a respect and support that is more likely to be reciprocated toward your program when freely given to theirs.

Outside Class Time

Busy music teachers often become so wrapped up in their multitude of tasks that they barely have a moment to leave the confines of their music room. And the few minutes they do take to dash to the staff room for a coffee or to the office for photocopies is sometimes done with blinders on—making a beeline for the destination somewhat oblivious to those around them.

Try to slow down long enough to notice students as you pass them in the hallways. Say hello and smile or have a quick chat. Make eye contact. It is important for your students to know that you see them and are interested in them as individuals both inside and outside your classroom. Remember that even if you don't know every student in the school, they know you, and it is important to represent yourself and your program in a student-friendly light. It doesn't take much effort to greet people as you pass by, but the more approachable you are, the more accessible your program will seem.

Music to Start the Day

Full-school music listening programs have been a wonderful way of making music education a part of everyone's day in many schools. For a few minutes at a regular time each day, staff and students can stop what they are doing and just listen. In the popular Brummitt-Taylor Music Listening Program (www.ttimbers.com/brummitt.htm), a single selection is played for a full school week, preceded each day by new information about the composer, performer, instrument, historical period and country, ensemble, or genre of music.

Listening programs can be a huge success in familiarizing students with music they would not normally hear outside school, and in teaching them about various aspects of the music and its creation. In addition, listening time often becomes a welcome break in the busyness of the academic day. Principals love to boast about innovative programs and inevitably they receive warm comments from parents and other visitors to the school about well-organized listening programs.

The tricky part about implementing a program of this sort is in gaining your principal's and colleagues' support in starting it up. Teachers are often reluctant, justifiably, to give up any of their class time for something unrelated to their own course material. And trying to keep students quiet to listen to music in between classes can be a daunting task.

The best option is to secure five minutes that is usually reserved for announcements or homeroom assembly. That way, you are not cutting into any curricular time, and are contributing to a positive start or end to the school day.

Some teachers may be skeptical or even unsupportive at first, and it is important for the music teacher to actively promote the program with colleagues as a time for quiet listening and reflection (a welcome change from the constant hum of activity that is ever-present in school classrooms). It may take a while to get everyone on board, but it is well worth the effort and will soon become a special part of the day that students and staff look forward to.

SUMMARY

Students are the lifeblood of every school and every program within the school. Students have an abundance of energy and ideas and want to be involved in meaningful experiences in their school. Music teachers need to tap into this energy, to involve students in the growth and development of their program, to reach out to those not presently involved and find ways to make programs more meaningful for all students.

Providing leadership opportunities is central to giving students a stake in the program. It allows opportunities for personal growth and for strengthening their dedication to the music program. Making music education fun by providing additional opportunities for socializing within ensembles and for additional learning experiences in camps and community ensembles helps develop a strong sense of cohesion and belonging as well as motivation for students to further their musical growth. Looking outside the program to those students who are passionate about music but have not yet found a voice within the school program, adding music as a component in every school member's day, and showing interest in students as individuals with many diverse interests will help to build a program with which students are proud to be affiliated.

ASSIGNMENTS

1. Research performing ensembles in and around the area in which you plan to teach. Do they give special shows for schools? Will they provide a sample CD so that you can judge their appropriateness for your program? How costly are live performances? Will they give special rates to schools? Are they available to perform during the school day? Will they perform at the school? Categorize the ensembles according to genre and performance medium. Highlight those ensembles you feel would best complement your program at high school, middle school, or elementary levels.

2. Brainstorm ideas for supporting gifted and talented students. Be realistic about the logistics of your ideas—how easily can they be implemented? You may wish to speak with a music teacher you respect—how does he or she support and provide learning experiences for these students? Discuss your ideas with him or her—how feasible are they?

3. Develop a rehearsal outline for section leaders. What will the general criteria and guidelines be? Will the students need to report to you regarding attendance, participation, and achievement of rehearsal goals? If so, create a template of the weekly report they will be asked to complete.

4. Make a plan for developing a student music committee at one school level (specify elementary, middle, or high school). How will it be structured? Will there be specific jobs for all or some students? Will you assign or have students elect a student leader, or will you serve as the leader? What will the role of the committee be? How will its responsibilities differ from those of the parent committee?

5. Develop a list of skills and activities that senior students can support or assist you with for younger grades. For instance, in an elementary school, how can sixth-grade students serve as models and mentors? In a high school, what leadership roles can the twelfth-grade music students fill?

6. Are there additional roles that pianists, guitarists, and other solo musicians can play in your school music program? How will you locate these students and encourage their participation in the school program?

7. Discuss with your classmates the issue of popular music in school music programs. What are the benefits and/or drawbacks to including this genre? Could and should entire programs be based on it? How can you see popular music being used effectively in an elementary, middle, or high school music program?

8. Research the summer music education opportunities in and around your region. What are the requirements for participation? What are the fees? Are they day camps or overnight camps? For what grade, achievement level, instruments, voices, or ensembles are they geared? If possible, collect brochures from each camp and save them for future reference. Are there some camps you would recommend to your students more than others? Why?

9. Research the available software for music education at the elementary, middle, or high school level. If possible, try the software or a demo version (often available online). Which programs would you like to purchase for your school program? Why? What is their overall purpose and design? Would you install it on laboratory computers or on the music room computer only? How much do these programs cost? Is there a special rate for schools?

Chapter 4

Performances

Performances are the primary vehicle through which most music programs are known. They are often the first, and sometimes the only, glimpse that the school and wider community have of what music education in your school is all about. While performance is certainly only a part of what music teachers and students do, it is nevertheless the component upon which judgments are often made with respect to the quality, value, and role of music education. This chapter focuses on a number of key issues pertaining to performances that can help raise the music program's profile and visibility in the school.

Performances can be very meaningful experiences for students. They offer an emotional outlet and an opportunity for participants to demonstrate and share with others the music they have worked hard to prepare. The desire to share music with others is inherent in the very nature of music making, and it is in performance opportunities that many students' passion and energy come to fruition. Other students' interest in music education is often piqued after attending a performance that has excited them. For these reasons, teachers need to find ways of making performance a more regular happening for their students than the standard twice-yearly concerts. This chapter focuses on a variety of ways to create performance opportunities both within and outside the school, as well as suggestions for making performances more memorable for audiences and participants alike.

SCHOOL CONCERTS

Entertaining Concerts

It is important for music teachers to think of concerts not only as venues in which to showcase their program, but also as entertaining events that are ideal for building positive public relations. Consider concerts as opportunities to let the whole school and parent population get to know you and your music program. When both parents work nine to five and/or music classes are optional, many audience members may not know you or even recognize you as the music teacher. This is your opportunity to let them see you as an interesting and approachable person—the type of teacher with whom they would like their children to work.

Take a minute or two at the beginning of the concert and in between sets to talk with the audience. You might tell them a little about the music department—its various offerings, performance groups, recent achievements and performances, and upcoming events. What would you like them to know about the particular selections that the students will be performing and the students who will be performing them? Are there any humorous anecdotes you could share about getting ready for the concert?

Spending a small amount of time communicating directly with your audience is a good strategy both for informing and presenting yourself and your program to them. It also breaks up the concert, providing a small amount of space in which to rest between musical offerings. The key is to be prepared and to keep speech to a minimum—otherwise you may lose your audience's focus and add unnecessarily to the concert length (which could result in people not staying for the full show).

Since music education is all about educating students, most of the selections they work on and perform should be material learned for its educational as well as its musical value. For concerts, it is often a good idea to also include a selection or two that the audience will recognize, or perhaps be invited to participate in by singing along or clapping. An occasional fun and interactive selection offers people a chance to stretch their muscles and move a little, and provides a brief reprieve from more serious and/or unfamiliar repertoire, however beautiful it may be. A small amount of audience participation can be a great strategy in maintaining interest and focus.

Intermission

If a concert is more than an hour in length, taking a small intermission is usually in order. This allows the audience and participants to catch their breath, socialize a little, and regain their focus for the remainder of the concert. Many schools make refreshments available for purchase at intermission, often as a fund-raiser for the music department. Parent committees are typically responsible for organizing concession stands for which treats are donated by parents or purchased from a bulk goods store.

If the proceeds are going to support a particular aspect of the program (for example, the annual orchestra or band trip, a new timpani, or new choir robes), there should be a sign to this effect. People like to know that their money is going to support a good cause and may be more inclined to make a purchase if they know what it is supporting. Informing the school community about the department's needs and activities is always a good strategy. You never know when there may be individuals present who are in a position to help.

Massed Ensembles

It can be a very powerful experience, for participants and audience alike, to conclude school concerts with one or two selections that incorporate the whole, or large portions of, the student body. These selections should be easy enough for the younger grades or less experienced musicians to manage, and appealing enough for all students to enjoy.

Songs are the usual candidates for massed ensembles, but coordinating several bands, band and orchestra, or uniting bands, orchestras, and choirs is certainly possible as well. You might consider having the band, guitar class, string, or Orff ensemble accompany a massed choir or play interludes between verses to create a cumulative end-of-show experience.

If you plan to include all students, even those not currently enrolled in music classes, you may wish to have a few sessions with those students to teach them their parts. Senior students and/or classroom teachers (if they are willing—this usually works well in elementary schools) can help review parts—providing a recording for them to work with is often helpful. The overall goal of a culminating massed-ensemble performance is for students and parents to leave the concert with a feeling of community inspired by the power of music.

Tickets

It can be beneficial on a number of fronts to charge a small admission fee to attend a school concert—but only if you live in a neighborhood where this is economically feasible for families (otherwise you will not only lose your audience, you will also exclude the community from the music-sharing experience).

The obvious reason for charging an admission fee is to raise funds for the music department. If, for example, there are seven hundred students in your school and each child has one parent in attendance (many will have two, plus aunts, uncles, and grandparents), in charging $2 per person (no fee for children) you will have raised $1,400. This sum can purchase fourteen or more band scores, six hundred or more choral octavos, or six or seven elementary musicals, thereby making a substantial contribution to your music budget. Keep in mind that any revenues from public performances of copyrighted music must be used for non-profit educational purposes (see www.menc.org/resources/view/copyright-center, "The United States Copyright Law: A Guide for Music-Educators".

A second reason to suggest an admission fee is that in modern society we tend to believe, whether consciously or not, that you get what you pay for. In other words, you might actually do yourself and your students a disservice if you do not charge admission. Selling tickets to see the show informs the audience that it is a show worth paying to see. Of course, if your community can afford to pay admission and you decide to go this route (and your school administration approves), do be sure that the concert is well organized and the students are well prepared. Perhaps that goes without saying—it will be high quality with or without the money!

Concert Halls

If your school does not have an auditorium in which to perform, concerts may normally be relegated to the school gym. It may be beneficial to instead consider renting a more formal facility for the event—the cost of which can often be covered by admission fees. The feasibility and appropriateness of doing so will depend on, among other factors, the economic position of your school community.

As is the case with selling tickets to the event, holding your performance in a concert hall signals to the community that you have a high-quality music program prepared to give a high-quality performance. As a bonus, seating is typically more comfortable and washrooms are larger and more parent-friendly than school gym facilities.

If it is feasible to do so, holding some performances in a hall can prove to be very valuable for your students. The acoustical properties of most halls are likely to be a vast improvement over those of the school gym. Performing under improved acoustical conditions allows students to experience a heightened awareness of balance, tuning, and overall musical effect. A great venue cannot, obviously, replace solid preparation, but it can enhance students' educational and performance experience. That being said, many fine and successful musicians have had their early performances in the school gym or church hall. Read on for suggestions about using these venues to their full potential.

The Gym

There are a variety of reasons why performances might be held in the school gym: among them, the expense or absence of an appropriate venue, the cost of rehearsal time and buses to the hall, or the loss of class time in transporting students to and from another venue to rehearse. Some teachers and school communities prefer to hold events in the school itself, simply because it reflects the life of the children.

Whether your reasons are financial-, time-, or preference-based, if you choose to hold your concerts in the school gym, consider it a priority to make this venue look its very best. The simplest way to do this is to call on your parent and/or student committee to help arrange the transformation (you will have enough to do with final musical preparations to worry about decorating).

In the spirit of the arts supporting each other, talk with the visual arts teacher about the possibility of displaying some student pieces in the foyer or on either side of the stage. The visibility can help to promote the art program, while turning the familiar school gym into a special performance venue. It is important to work with the art teacher in this regard, so that the displays are truly representative of the art department and the students' skills and achievements. To do otherwise might risk demeaning the work of a fellow arts teacher and his or her students, not to mention damaging a valuable collegial relationship.

In addition to artwork, you might like to place pots or vases of flowers along the front of the stage—parents are often willing to donate them, either purchased or fresh from their garden. You might prefer to borrow flowers or plants from around the school, or ask a local florist for donations (remember to thank contributors in the program).

If the seating is on the gym floor, rather than on risers, arranging it in a neat and attractive way that allows all sides to have the best possible view should be a priority. Dividing the gym into three sections with the two outside sections angled toward the stage and the middle section facing the stage is often a good layout.

Students can help with decorations by cutting out brightly colored flowers, stars, music notes, fir trees, or other appropriate or seasonal images, to hang on the walls of the gym. Check to see if your school has an Ellison machine, which can cut many shapes quickly, neatly, and uniformly—then you can enlist students to simply hang them. A backdrop adds a certain touch of elegance and formality to the event—if your school doesn't have one, and you have funds available (they can be pricey), you might consider renting one. It can be the finishing touch in preparing a special venue in which your students can share their musical achievements with the school community. No matter the approach you take or the materials you use to decorate, the idea is to transform the space visually and psychologically from a basketball court into a performance venue.

Beginning-Level Ensembles

It is vitally important to encourage and motivate young musicians from the outset of their training. While much of this encouragement occurs during class and rehearsal time, the key to keeping students interested in practicing and performing at their best is to provide them with opportunities to perform. Unfortunately, in school concerts, beginning ensembles, with their limited skills and repertoire choices, are generally allotted the least amount of time.

A solution to this dilemma is to find or create additional performance opportunities, especially for the beginning ensembles. This affords students the opportunity to demonstrate what they have learned to an appreciative audience—their parents, teachers, and one or two younger grades (who may be inspired to join up when their time comes). You might have the students perform selections for full ensemble, interspersed with selections highlighting individual sections or small groups.

When planning an event like this with a limited audience, it is a good idea to look for a venue that is roughly the right size and avoid using one that is too large where many seats will be empty (I have held my fifth-grade band concert outside on the lawn on sunny May days). It is also important to make the concert as official as possible to make it clear that a great deal of work went into preparing for it and, although the students are beginners, the performances should be respected and taken seriously. The national anthem, played or sung by one of the students, and a few words from the principal usually set the tone.

A reception after the performance serves as a celebration of the students' achievement and hard work throughout the year. You might enlist the help of the participating grades' classroom teachers to set it up. Often the music department can provide drinks (tea, coffee, and juice/bottled water) and parents can donate treats. A reception is an excellent opportunity for you and your students' parents to become better acquainted in a positive environment—following a successful concert highlighting their children's achievements.

A beginners-only concert can be highly motivating for students and a wonderful opportunity for parents to get a better sense of what their children have been learning. The importance you place on beginning level students (instead of focusing your attention on more advanced groups) is clear and much appreciated. In my experience, this has been a turning point for some parents in their all-out support for the music program.

Video Recordings

Hire a professional or, better yet, look for professionals among the parent body to record school performances. By documenting your musical events you can create a program portfolio—a tangible record of the music program for years to come. Parents are usually happy to purchase a video of their child on stage, which can also help to build support both financially and practically for the music program. Be sure to read through the MENC Copyright Centre website (www.menc.org/resources/view/copyright-center/copyr.html#school) before making more than one copy of a concert recording, as permission is required from the publishers to do so, and royalties will normally need to be paid.

Uniforms

It is vital to build a sense of community among your students and unity within performing groups. Uniforms are a simple, yet effective means of visually tying a group together and providing a psychological sense of unity among the performers. Since the number of schools requiring daily uniforms is relatively few in the public system, music teachers need to be creative in finding ways of achieving this unity for their performances.

Schools with substantial music budgets and/or higher-income families may be able to purchase choir robes or band and orchestra uniforms—there are many beautiful options from which to choose. However, these uniforms can be costly, and there are more economical, yet equally effective, ways of achieving the same end. Many teachers find that the simplest option is to have everyone wear black bottoms and white tops.

Another approach is to have everyone wear black bottoms and a top in a single color family (different shades of red or blue, for example, work well in achieving unity and interest at the same time). Some teachers ask students to wear any solid color shirt they wish (still keeping a single color on bottom), which can also work nicely in achieving an appearance of ensemble. Other teachers get creative with scarves, hats, or other items that help to create an appearance of unity for the audience, as well as contribute to a feeling of unity among the musicians themselves.

ADDITIONAL SCHOOL PERFORMANCES

Musicals

Whether you teach at the elementary or secondary level there is a wide variety of appealing musicals available to suit student skills, interests, and abilities. You will have no trouble finding students who want to be involved in a musical production, and there are many ways to tap into student talent and interest: lead roles, chorus, backstage, makeup, costumes, scenery, promotion, ushering, and so on.

You will find that students who are not otherwise involved in the music program often come out to be a part of a musical. And, as a bonus, students who get turned on to music through the school musical will often become regular members of other aspects of the music program. You may even uncover hidden talents—the second-clarinetist with the previously undiscovered dynamite voice.

Musicals can help build a sense of community, student morale, and allegiance to the music department. As well, they provide great opportunities for engaging other teachers in musical endeavors. Many teachers are happy to help with promoting a musical, supervising prop creation, makeup, and so on. The more you involve nonarts teachers in arts productions, the more they will come to understand the value of the program and the complexity of what students are learning.

Musicals have fantastic public relations capabilities. Parents who are not particularly comfortable with the traditional band-orchestra-choir setting tend to find musicals more accessible. If you perform a big-name musical like *Grease, Annie,* or *Jesus Christ Superstar,* there is an added bonus of promoting your program throughout the wider community. People not affiliated with your school will often come to see a performance of a well-known show, especially if professional shows are not normally produced in or near your town.

Musicals are inevitably a lot of work, and copyright laws need to be strictly observed (see www.menc.org/resources/view/copyright-center), but they can pay dividends in creating a sense of community among your students, rallying the school community around your program, and putting your school music program on the local map.

Dinner Theatre

One of the most intriguing and innovative strategies I have heard of lately for fund- and profile-raising is to hold a full-fledged dinner theatre. The fact that I heard about the idea from an acquaintance with no ties to music education whatsoever is testimony to its success in bringing music to the attention of the community.

You can build a performance around an existing musical, perhaps a reduction, or have students work in conjunction with the drama department to create an original work. The food can be either catered or specially prepared by kitchen staff. Parents and students can help turn the gym or other large room into a dining room using lighting, candles, tablecloths, curtains, and artwork. The size of the audience and the cost of the catering and décor will factor into how much you should charge for tickets, but for dinner and theatre you should be able to charge enough to cover expenses plus a little extra for the department.

Of course, the economic situation of the school community will have to be considered—if parents cannot feasibly pay $50 a head to attend, then it would be self-defeating to ask that amount. Having to cancel a performance would be discouraging for students, and putting too much financial pressure on otherwise supportive families might embarrass them and ultimately diminish their overall participation. Keeping the economics of the school community in mind during the planning stage will help you to plan an evening that is cost effective and still serves to bring your students and program to the attention of the school community.

Celebrations

Grade celebrations to close out a successful school year are particularly important for students at the elementary and middle school levels. Classroom teachers are often happy to help plan the event for their grade. The program will likely include a variety of material, illustrating different facets of their music class: songs, student compositions, dances, Orff arrangements, recorder ensemble selections, demonstrations of mapped listening experiences, or short musical plays (perhaps composed by the children themselves).

It is best to keep the program reasonably short (twenty to forty minutes) so that you have time for a reception and make it possible for parents to attend during the school day. Last block in the day is usually a good time as children have to be picked up anyway—parents can often arrange to come a little earlier to take part in the event.

You will need to reserve a room large enough to support the performers, parents, and possibly some of the younger classes. It is very important to round off the event with some food and drink. A reception gives a sense of completion and builds an awareness that the students' achievements in music are important and should be feted. Receptions also give parents a chance to chat with each other and with you—in both cases the topic of conversation will likely center about the children's musical achievements. For the little extra work involved in planning grade celebrations, they can increase understanding, pride, and support for your music program while making it a visibly integral component of the school.

Foyer Performances

Practically every school has a main foyer—an open space at the entrance to the building where people can meet and greet on their way into school. This is often the perfect area in which to acquaint the school community with your talented young performers on a regular basis. If you have a piano that can be permanently situated in the foyer, so much the better, as it will allow your young pianists and accompanied singers and instrumentalists to perform.

Providing a regular performance time each week in this informal venue can work effectively at all school levels. Students who take private instruction on an instrument, who are learning independently, or who are learning through the school program can all be offered an opportunity to play or sing, alone or in a small ensemble, for their school community. Try to project which time of day will work best in your school—perhaps in the morning while teachers, parents, and students are entering the building, or at lunchtime when students and staff often have a little downtime. Student performances make a pleasant change from the ordinary routine. Students, teachers, and parents enjoy hearing from the young talents in the school and will often stop for a few minutes to listen.

If your school is very large, the foyer may not be the best place for students to perform. With too many students entering the building at once it can be difficult for the performers to be heard, and equally difficult to keep the others quiet without having to "police" the area, which would certainly take away from the experience as a positive one. In this case, you may want to look for a somewhat more intimate setting within the school that still allows for your young performers to be seen and heard without being overwhelmed or drowned out by the masses.

Providing regular performance opportunities gives students a chance to hone their performing skills and build confidence. It also demonstrates the strength of your music program and reminds the school community of the music department's presence on a regular basis. Be sure to post the names of the performers, the compositions, and the composers in the performance area so that others can know who and what they are listening to.

Singing Telegrams

Singing telegrams are a unique offering of choral programs to the overall spirit of the school community. For special events like birthdays or Valentine's Day, small choral ensembles can be dispatched to relay a singing message to a friend or significant other. Any combination of voices can work—four-part, two-part, even unison can work well, provided the ensemble is well-prepared and the students are confident performers. Select some short, fun, and popular tunes to be recycled from occasion to occasion and find a place in the song to insert the recipient's name.

While singing telegrams have been more commonly heard in high schools, they can be used equally effectively by late elementary and middle school students. No matter the age level, you will want to ensure that the students involved can sing correctly, in tune, and in a confident and secure manner. While the recipients will enjoy their efforts and the telegrams are meant to add to the school environment in a fun and joyful manner, there is no room for performers who behave poorly, do not take the job seriously, or who cannot perform for an audience at close range. Students who wish to take part need to understand that relaying a singing message on behalf of another person is serious business—in particular when payment is required to send the message.

Telegrams make a great and novel way to raise funds for the music department. For a small fee, students or teachers can purchase a telegram for a friend, teacher, or other staff member. This is a great way of contributing to the community life and spirit of your school, making music education directly relevant to students' lives, reinforcing the value of music in education, and simply reminding the school of your department's presence and value.

The National Anthem

If your music department is not currently responsible for starting off school and sporting events with the national anthem, you might consider making it a new priority. And not just for the big concerts—let the anthem open your school assemblies, smaller performances, and athletic events as well. Why? First of all, it will help to ensure that your young musicians and the entire school community know the national anthem. Secondly, it provides frequent opportunities in which to highlight your musicians—soloists and small ensembles, male and female, instrumental and vocal. By having your students contribute to school events, musical and otherwise, you can highlight the excellence of your program and demonstrate its relevance to school and community life.

Student Performances

It is hard to build up a support base for something that is kept private. When students study music privately and practice diligently in their home environment, it sometimes remains a relatively private endeavor if their classmates and teachers never have the opportunity to see or hear them perform.

You can easily arrange for in-class performances once every month or two. You might even reserve five or ten minutes each week in which to let students perform for the class. Providing regular performance opportunities can be beneficial to all students and to your overall program. It helps build the performers' comfort in performing, gives them opportunities in which to try out repertoire for an audience, and allows them to show what they have achieved on the instrument or with their voice. It gives them recognition for their effort and achievement and helps to build their self-esteem and pride in being a young musician.

For the students who do not perform, it opens their eyes to possibilities and may prompt them to ask for lessons themselves. It also helps them to understand what their friends have been working on in the privacy of their homes, thereby raising their opinion of musical study. For all the children, it provides an opportunity to learn how to be a good audience member and a supportive classmate.

On a practical level, these performance opportunities inform you about which students are involved in music instruction outside school time. You will want to keep track of how these students are progressing and what their achievements are in order to find ways of incorporating them into your program and to let their achievements be known throughout the school. You might occasionally need student performers for various events. Knowing who's out there allows you to invite appropriately prepared individuals rather than risk putting out a call for which no one or inadequately prepared students may respond. Knowing which students are enrolled in private lessons also informs you of a body of parents who value music education. They are likely to be advocates for music education and are key candidates for your parent committee.

School Functions

In the course of the school year there are numerous social events for which the music department can make a valuable contribution. Find out what these events are and how you can help. School assemblies are great forums for promoting your department. Have the jazz band, string orchestra, concert band, or show choir provide an official opening and closing to the event. Smaller ensembles can perform for parent coffee mornings; guitar, recorder, or small combos can play during open houses. Perhaps your students can perform a scene from the upcoming musical. Have a sing-a-long at the annual Santa's Breakfast. Prepare commemorative and reflective music for Veteran's Day/Remembrance Day events. For Mother's Day celebrations, have your choir perform a song of appreciation.

Ask your colleagues what kind of special occasions they may be having within their classes or grades, and think about how you might be able to contribute with a musical element. At every opportunity, provide musical components for school events. Once you've started the tradition, it will be hard for anyone to imagine a time before music was an integral part of the school life. The key to appreciation of music programs is to immerse the program in the school community. You can make it an essential component.

Meetings

Parents, teachers, and school administrators all have a variety of responsibilities that require meetings from time to time. While dealing with important school and student issues, these meetings can, at times, be tedious and tense. As the resident music teacher, why not offer a brief overture to liven things up? A short performance (five minutes—tops) by a small ensemble (so setup and takedown are quick and minimal) can start the meeting off on a pleasant note and remind all involved about the value of music education—it contributes to life!

Use every available occasion to remind parents and administrators of your existence. It is too easy to overlook programs that you see only two times a year, at the winter and spring concerts. Let your chamber choir sing a song or two at the start of the PTA meeting, have your jazz band play a few tunes at the next board meeting. Go one step further and find a way of performing for the department of education or the teachers' union.

Aside from informing these audiences about the skills and achievements of your students, you will be reminding them of the importance of maintaining high-quality arts programs in the schools: you are rounding out their children's education, helping them to develop into well-rounded, complete people. And you can achieve this all while setting up a relaxed atmosphere in which to meet, adding interest to what could potentially be another run-of-the-mill meeting.

On a practical note, if equipment is involved that would require more than a few minutes to set up and take down, you should inquire about the best place to do this so that you can prepare before the meeting starts and take down after it is over or the next day (just be sure that the area is secure if you plan to leave equipment overnight).

Teacher Performances

If you want to inspire your students to strive for a higher level of achievement, one of the best things you can do is to let them hear what a higher level looks and sounds like. There are a number of options for live musical experiences, but the simplest, most consistent, and perhaps most effective, is for *you* to play or sing for them.

Your students have already built up a relationship with you and many likely see you as a role model, since music teachers tend to have a special bond with many of their students. Let them hear you play or sing. You can do this in a very unassuming way by demonstrating music concepts in class, sitting in with a section from time to time, and playing between classes while students are coming in or leaving. You might decide to play as part of a growing ensemble to help raise the resultant quality, thereby heightening students' overall satisfaction in the ensemble. Or you might decide to give a more formal performance, alone or in collaboration with other musicians. It is so valuable for students to hear high-level playing, especially from someone who is real to them, someone they already know and respect.

Events for Student-Run Ensembles

In addition to opening practice space to student-run ensembles, you might consider holding a "battle of the bands" type of event, which tends to be both high energy and high profile. Depending on the number of ensembles, you might need to audition prior to the actual event in order to keep the program at a reasonable length. You might even extend invitations to neighboring schools to make it a higher profile community event. Because of the predominance of student groups during the high school years, this event is generally best geared toward secondary programs, although occasionally select middle schools also find a number of student groups among their population.

Aside from booking the venue, making sure that the sound equipment is ready, and possibly auditioning ensembles, the work for you is actually much less than with a traditional concert. Students will be keen to take the event on as their own—from setting up decorations to concessions, even preparing programs, much of the work can be done by students.

Your fellow teachers will likely be enthusiastic about seeing their students perform with ensembles they have put together on their own. Often these events reveal talented students not currently involved in the school music program, who should be encouraged to consider the various in-school options. You may find that a composition or vocal skills class, for example, would be very exciting options that students may not have known about, considered, or thought accessible—particularly if they are self-taught musicians. You may find some of your most creative and passionate students in the school's so-called "garage bands."

Performances by student-run groups sometimes also uncover gifted musicians who have not been successful academically (of course, you will also find some who are great academic students) and some who are not involved in school-organized extra-curricular activities. It is extremely gratifying for teachers to see these students achieving in one area of their life and receiving positive attention for it. This can be a great confidence booster for the students, but it also takes a great deal of confidence for them to pluck up their courage and perform in front of their peers and teachers.

Students generally recognize the fact that these performances are not easy for their peers to give and they tend to be incredibly supportive of each other. Parents, too, are very keen to see their children perform and be recognized for something that they work on in the privacy of their own home. The good publicity these types of events bring can raise the profile of the music department as well, making it a win-win situation for all involved.

OUTSIDE THE SCHOOL

The Bigger Picture

Consider involving your students in large-scale projects that connect them to the wider musical community. Events such as a school districts' "Spring Sing," MENC's "World's Largest Concert," or the Coalition for Music Education's (Canada) "Music Monday" involve huge numbers of students from many different schools either locally or nationally. Avail yourself and your students of such opportunities to see and hear the bigger picture and to realize that there are vast numbers of students everywhere equally involved in music. Your students will have the opportunity for music making on a large scale, which can be a very powerful experience.

It can be beneficial for your school to be seen at and associated with these types of events. It demonstrates that you are in touch with the music community and that you have built up a program that is on par with others in the community and across the country. When parents and administrators attend such events they are often overwhelmed by the experience and leave with a new and positive perspective on the value of music education.

Charity Events

There are countless worthy charitable organizations today—most of which periodically hold fund-raising breakfasts, brunches, and dinners. Very often these events are spiced up with a little musical entertainment. If you have a staff or parent connection to such an organization you can express your interest in performing through them. Otherwise, place a phone call and offer your services. Consider it another performance opportunity for your students—a chance for them to hone their repertoire and their performance skills, to enjoy performing for an appreciative audience, and to let your school name be recognized in connection with music education.

Television fund-raisers frequently have guest performers. And while you might not make it on PBS, there may be local events looking for more local talent. Telethons in aid of children's hospitals, in particular, are ideal venues for school groups since they focus on young people. Keep your eyes and ears open for upcoming events on your local television station. A spot on TV would be fantastic PR for your music department and would serve to raise your profile within the school as well as in the wider community.

Music Educators' Conferences

Music educators' conferences occur at several different levels: provincial/state, regional, national, and international levels. At each level, student groups are solicited to perform. What great opportunities to showcase your program to others in your profession! Acceptance at a conference is a major achievement, clearly underlining the high quality of your program. Performing at one would give your students the opportunity to hear other high-level groups and perform as their equal, which can be a real eye-opener for many.

On a public relations level, being seen and heard at a conference lets your school name be known on a much wider level as a school with a high-quality music program. It brings a certain status and prestige that will make it difficult for administrators thinking of cutting or reducing your program to actually do so.

The Community

To bring your program to the attention of the wider community, it is essential that you physically incorporate it into community life. Find opportunities for classes and ensembles to perform at venues outside the school. Shopping centers are good bets, but don't wait until the holiday season when they are actively looking for performers. Phone the manager and offer to bring your ensemble in on a weekday or weekend any time of the year. More often than not, he or she will be delighted to take you up on your offer—it will provide entertainment for customers and show that the center supports community initiatives. Besides, if students are performing, you can bet that a number of moms and dads will find their way to the venue as well (and will probably end up doing a little shopping once the show is over . . .).

Hospitals and senior citizens' homes are wonderful places for students to perform. Patients and residents love to have a little entertainment, especially in the form of school-age children. Often, seniors' homes will invite the students to mingle and have tea with the residents after performing, which can be a unique learning experience for the children and a meaningful one for the residents. In performing this outreach service, your students will also have an opportunity to perform in public, perhaps as a practice run for a more formal performance, and your school name and music program will come to the attention of the wider community.

Additionally, in each of these environments there are a myriad of diverse individuals in addition to your intended audience who will get to see and hear your students: nurses, doctors, cafeteria staff, X-ray technicians, and various other medical and administrative staff who work in the home or hospital. Performing in such venues promotes your school name and program throughout the community.

Public gardens and market-squares, parks, coffee shops, and outdoor shopping districts are also possible venues for performances. Open your mind to the possibilities and place a few calls. It doesn't take much effort to ask and the payoffs in student achievement and public recognition can be substantial.

Competitions and Festivals

There may be no better way to put your school name on the map than to make a good showing at music festivals and competitions. This is where teachers, parents, and students from other schools get to see you and your students in action and learn to associate your school name with excellence in music. Music festivals can be a great learning experience and motivator.

Having a festival to work toward can inspire students to put extra effort into their practice and rehearsals. The additional outside-of-school performance opportunity helps to hone their performance skills and gives them the satisfaction that comes from sharing their music with others. The feedback they receive from adjudicators can help to improve their skills (and often support what you have been working on in class). And the opportunity to hear, and sometimes meet, students from other schools can be both educational and motivational.

However, festivals can also have negative effects. An adjudicator who is overly critical or not sympathetic to the sensibilities of young people can spoil the good that the experience had to offer. Performing in a competition for which students are ill prepared, or of a standard that they are simply not ready for, can be devastating, as the students hear and are compared against groups that far exceed their own skill level. Focusing on a goal of winning, placing, or attaining a gold status puts the wrong emphasis on the event and sets students up for feeling as though they have failed, should the results prove to be not as high as they had anticipated. The key is for the teacher—who sometimes must also educate parents and colleagues—to approach the festival in a manner that reflects the educational benefits.

Whether your students are performing at a very high level already or are just starting to work as an ensemble, you can find festivals appropriate for their level. There are festivals at local, state, national, and international levels that school groups around the continent participate in every year. When first approaching the festival circuit, you will probably want to start at the local level—possibly with a noncompetitive event. That way, students reap the positive benefits while avoiding the win-lose possibility. Some festivals offer competitive and noncompetitive classes, so you could potentially start with the noncompetitive and move toward competitive classes as your groups progress. Or you may want to start by bringing a select group to a small ensemble festival and progress toward bringing your large ensembles once they are more established.

No matter what type of festival you choose or which ensembles you bring, repertoire selection is always the key to a successful performance— always making sure that the pieces you choose are challenging enough to improve students' skills, but accessible enough for them to perform well. Do not use competitions as a means to push your students to a performance level that they are not ready for—this will simply place undue stress on everyone involved and may result in weak performance, poor morale, and students dropping out of the program.

It is important to let your students know what to expect at the festival— how the whole thing works—from the warm-ups to the order of selections, from waiting between selections to the final comments from adjudicators. Be sure to prepare your students for the possibility of critical judges. Remind them of how much they have achieved, how well they are doing, and how proud you are of them.

Explain the process whereby adjudicators provide comments about things that are really good in the performance, as well as things they can do to be even better. Let them know that occasionally an adjudicator assumes that students already know what they are doing well and therefore only focus on things that need improvement. This prepares students for the possibility of an overly critical judge. The last thing you want when taking kids out to perform is to have their spirits broken by a negative assessment.

The more students perform in public, including performances at competitive and noncompetitive festivals, the more confidence and pride they will gain in their skills. If approached with an eye toward motivating and educating, keeping in mind the above suggestions, these events can be wonderful learning opportunities that also help to promote your program within and outside the school.

SUMMARY

Performance is central to music education. The potential for sharing musical expression and experience is a powerful motivator for many students and a powerful community builder for schools. The key is to provide opportunities for students to have a variety of performance experiences and to make them accessible and enjoyable for the school and wider community. Formal concerts, informal foyer performances, grade celebrations, and battle of the bands all provide such opportunities and contribute greatly to the life of your program and the overall life of the school.

ASSIGNMENTS

1. Research large-scale musical events at the local, state/provincial, and national levels. Contact music education organizations at each level for information on how to get your school involved. If you find that no such events happen in your area, what can you envision for the future? How could it be organized? Would you be willing to get things started? How would you go about doing so?
2. Brainstorm local or regional charity and public events and venues at which your students might perform. Would performances at any school level be appropriate in each situation or are some more relevant for one level than another?
3. Make a list of songs that would work well as singing telegrams for a given school level. Select one to arrange for this purpose and perform it with two or three classmates for your class.
4. Research the financial and legal details behind performing a large-scale musical. How are fees charged? What type of advertising can you do? How many performances can you give? What other administrative details are important to know before embarking on such a project?
5. For class discussion:
    a. Discuss with your classmates the statement "You get what you pay for" with respect to school concerts. What are the advantages and/or disadvantages to charging a fee?
    b. Discuss the issue of venue for school concerts. What are your thoughts about keeping performances on school grounds or moving them off school grounds? What options are available in your area?
6. Writing assignment:
    a. Write a memo to your fellow teachers offering musical contributions for special events. Give examples of the types of events you

would be willing to help with. Ask them to let you know in advance so you have time to prepare. Do they want a particular ensemble, their own class, grade, or level to perform? Make your memo upbeat and encouraging. Let them know you have an important program that you are willing and ready to share in creating a positive school environment.

b. Write a letter as in the assignment above, directed this time to your school administrators, offering musical contributions for meetings and other events.

Chapter 5

Courses

For many classically trained music teachers, the core of the music program centers about the concert band, orchestra, or choir. This is indeed the model that most often comes to mind with respect to music education—at least at the middle and high school levels. Without a doubt, these ensembles are very valuable components of music education; however, they may not meet the needs and interests of the entire student body—rather, they often serve only a select few.

There are a number of options for diversifying music education such that more students are aware of and engaged in a variety of valuable, meaningful music-learning experiences. Together with suggestions for recording and acknowledging student achievement and ideas for building skills through support programs and events, this will be the focus of the present chapter.

DOCUMENTING SUCCESS

Course Outlines

Prepare detailed course outlines for each course that you teach, including topics to be covered, expectations of students, and grading procedures. Post them outside your room for all to see and send them home with students. By making your expectations clear from the outset, students and parents will be aware of your expectations and grading structure, leaving no room for surprises at reporting time.

Providing outlines at the beginning of the year depicts you as a teacher who is highly organized, detail- and goal-oriented, and who knows his or her material thoroughly. Course outlines also help to provide structure for the year. They require you to think through the course plan before it begins and make important decisions about texts, repertoire, concepts, competitions, festivals, and trips.

In addition to providing cohesion and structure to your courses, outlines provide the school community with a sense of what takes place in your classroom and what is involved in the particular course. Because music teachers have such an ingrained understanding of music education techniques and learning outcomes, they sometimes forget that most people do not have a complete understanding of what is involved in music classes. For example, with respect to choral music education, the image is typically of groups of students singing together while following a conductor. However, the details of learning to sing correctly in parts, with a good tone, proper breath support and diction, while interpreting musical indications, blending with their section, and sometimes even working in foreign languages are not at the forefront of most people's minds.

Your job, as a dedicated music teacher, is to let them know. Your class involves many complex activities that, combined, make for good choral singing. By giving the school community an awareness of what your courses entail they will have a basis upon which to value it as it should be valued.

Video Camera

The purchase of a department video camera can be an important acquisition in its growth. Consider using some of your fund-raising money to buy one (and a tripod)—the cost, compared with the payoff, will be minimal.

Uses for a video camera in a school music department are varied. When polishing repertoire selections, you might tape a rehearsal and use it to visually and aurally demonstrate the current state of the performance, so students more clearly understand what needs to be done to make it better. After working on the material, tape it again to show the improvement.

When assessing students' skills, a video camera can be particularly handy. Set it up in a practice room and let students tape their playing one at a time while you continue a full rehearsal. This arrangement can be beneficial on a number of fronts. First, you don't have to lose valuable rehearsal time to run tests. Second, it may reduce students' level of performance anxiety since they are not performing in front of you or their classmates. Third, it gives you an opportunity to take time in assessing students' achievements and, most importantly, to determine the cause of problems in their playing or singing. Finally, a videotape can serve as a tangible record of students' achievement—a challenging but important thing for music teachers to obtain. Any parent concerns or disputes about grades can be met with objective evidence of skills.

Additionally, video cameras can be used to record student performances at both school and outside venues. Taping of competition performances can be very useful in illustrating adjudicators' comments (some competitions videotape every performance along with running adjudicator comments). Plus, it can be wonderful to have a record of individual and program development over the years—when your students are getting ready to graduate you might want to arrange a viewing party of their musical and performance growth over the years.

VARIETY

Beyond Band, Orchestra, and Choir

If you want to build the music profile within your school, you need to have a program that appeals to a wide range of student interests and abilities—particularly at the high school level. While the traditional band/orchestra/choir model at the middle and high school levels is an engaging and exciting option for some students, the percentage of the overall student body who typically participates in these ensembles is generally small. Yet we know that music is an important part of most people's lives—in particular during the adolescent years. So why are music courses not filled to overflowing in our schools?

There are a number of reasons why students may opt out of the traditional ensemble based courses. It is a sad fact that there is a wide disparity in music education offerings across the country—from exceptional to nonexistent. As a result, some students enter high school with limited or no music education. These students may not feel comfortable with, or capable of, joining a band, string, or choral program. While many schools have an open choir that would accept students with no experience, it is not always possible to find a band or orchestral program for beginners at the upper school levels. Other students may not be able to afford fees that are sometimes associated with ensemble programs for instrument rentals and other costs. And while many schools have systems in place to support students in financial need, not all students are willing to let their need be known and so opt to simply not participate.

Some students steer clear of the arts in favor of a math/science model that they (and their parents) believe adds a certain rigor to their college applications. Other students are very interested in music, but not interested in playing and/or performing it. Still other students have no experience with or understanding of traditional forms and styles of music and therefore find traditional ensembles to be outside their realm of interest.

If music education is to truly be for all students, we have to find ways to interest and engage all students in courses that fit their needs, skills, and interests. The more appealing your program is to a broader range of students, the more likely it is that numbers of participants in the overall program will grow. As more students, parents, and administrators become aware of and involved in your music program, the more the relevance of music education in students' lives will be understood and the stronger your base of support will become. The suggestions for courses that follow pertain primarily to the high school level, although some options may be feasible at the middle level or as a component of an elementary program.

Jazz Band and Show Choir

Ensembles that are seen as contemporary and fun not only attract student interest, they also catch the attention of parents and administrators. The nature of such ensembles, with popular and upbeat music and, in the case of show choir, colorful and appealing costumes and choreography, make them attractive to the general public. The parental and community support for these types of ensembles often transfers easily to other components of the music program.

While jazz band and show choir are certainly not new to the high school scene, some teachers make the mistake of focusing primarily on building traditional ensembles while pouring less energy into these more contemporary, audience-friendly styles. If approached from a pedagogical standpoint, all types of ensembles can be sound learning grounds for developing musicians. It only makes good business sense to include ensembles in the roster that can contribute to the overall success and support of the department.

Guitar Class

While traditional instruments and ensembles are considered by some to have a high-society stigma attached to them, the guitar has not suffered under this impression. Next to the piano, the guitar is likely to be the most common instrument found in North American homes. At parties, around campfires, and at summer camps, guitars tend to be associated with music that everyone can relate to, that people grow up with and understand. Students who may never be interested in joining the school band or choir may find guitar class an exciting opportunity.

Mastering the guitar is, of course, no easier than mastering any other instrument. However, skill in playing just a few chords will allow students the freedom to accompany many popular songs, which can bring a great deal of musical satisfaction. And the desire to be able to do this can be a great motivator in overcoming any technical hurdles.

Adding a guitar class to your curriculum can diversify your program, enabling you to reach a wider body of students than through a strictly traditional program. Guitars can also broaden the department's appeal with parents who may see the guitar as a more accessible and relevant instrument to learn.

As an added bonus, by teaching students to play the guitar, you will be strengthening the overall musicianship of your community. It is more likely that students will continue to play the guitar once they graduate than it is for most other instruments, for which ensemble participation and repertoire has been the primary vehicle for musical satisfaction. The guitar is accessible and portable and allows students to achieve a degree of musical satisfaction relatively early in the learning process.

Piano Class

Piano class is becoming a popular choice in schools from elementary through secondary levels. Piano, like guitar, is an instrument that many students are interested in playing, and laboratory classes are viewed as more progressive and less daunting than the traditional one-on-one approach. There is an initial outlay of money that needs to be available to set up a lab at first, so unless you can convince your principal to foot the bill, it might be necessary to plan a few years in advance to raise funds for the purchase. School administrators and parents (and students) like piano labs because they link the arts with technology, which is a hot seller in today's academic marketplace.

There are plenty of resources available for piano class instruction and many ways the instruments can be used—from basic keyboarding skills to theory, ear training, improvisation, and composition lessons. Their versatility makes them particularly well suited for schools that cover a broad range of grades, and the purchase can be more easily justified when more students avail themselves of them.

At the secondary level, you may find that students who opted out of band, orchestra, and choir readily join a piano class. You will also find students signing up who dropped out of traditional piano lessons, but are still interested in learning to play the instrument. At the upper school levels, you may want to hold auditions to determine students' playing level—or lack thereof—so that students can be grouped together most effectively.

The great thing about piano labs is that, because students work with headsets and the teacher can move between instruments either by using the teacher console or by physically moving throughout the room, you can have students with a wide variety of skill levels working simultaneously on very different material. This makes any given class workable for students with and without prior experience on the instrument, thereby opening up a viable course option for all students.

Composition and Songwriting

Music technology has made composing and songwriting more accessible than ever. The use of electronic keyboards and computer software allows students to write music that they can hear as they compose it, and notate it without necessarily having a strong background in music theory or harmony. They can play with instrumentation, cut, paste, print, and record their works all with the click of a mouse. A composition course might include components such as teaching how to use the software and keyboard, traditional theory and arranging/orchestration lessons, musical form, introducing instrumental timbres, analysis of instrumental compositions and/or songs, and recording and preparing works for performance.

Such a course would be appealing for many students who are currently involved in the music program as well as many who are not. Many students are already involved in songwriting in the privacy of their own homes—with their guitar, pianos/keyboards, and garage bands. Why not help students focus their creative skills in the context of a structured and well-balanced course? It would certainly be an appealing option and addition to your overall program.

Sound Recording

This may not be as unrealistic as you think. Modern technology makes it possible to have good quality equipment at relatively low costs. Students can learn to work sound boards and lay down tracks. You can focus on aural skills as a necessary component of effective recording skills. Students can work with peers in performance classes to practice what they've learned in class.

If you do not have any experience with recording technology, try to recruit assistance from someone who does—a former classmate from college, a friend who works in the industry or plays with a band, a parent, a fellow teacher, or another music teacher at your school or in the community. Or, work with the education representative from a reputable music equipment manufacturer.

Recording systems in schools are getting to be more and more common, and sales reps know what you will require to fit your needs as well as where to start in order to fit your budget. They can also give you training in how to use the equipment. A sound recording course makes a very nice addition to the music roster—mixing music skills with technology. The equipment can serve double duty as a means of recording your students for auditions and competition preliminary rounds, and as a learning and assessment tool.

Garage Band

The traditional approach to music education has largely avoided working with popular music in general and popular-style groups in particular. "Garage" bands have been viewed as just that—bands that students run out of their parents' garages without teacher support or supervision. All the musical skills and nuances are worked out through trial and error by the individuals and groups involved.

Students who play in their own bands often gain a great deal of popularity. Their bands are supported proudly by classmates in battle-of-the-band events, and they are sometimes called upon to play at school events such as dances and proms. While often very talented and dedicated to their art, many of these students never take part in traditional music education nor are they supported by their school music program.

Why not consider offering a garage band course? All the same basics apply to working with a popular ensemble as to working with a traditional one—only the instruments and music are different. Instrumental and vocal skills need to be honed; balance and blend need to achieved; the ability to work with multiple parts happening at the same time is essential; the understanding of harmony and the use of ear training skills are essential to success in working out parts that are often learned by ear from recordings rather than from notated scores. Students could bring their own instruments and equipment or, if funds are available, you could purchase a limited number of guitars, basses, keyboards, and amplifiers in the same way that you would purchase school trumpets and clarinets.

Such a course has the potential to broaden the appeal of the music program to a wider range of students and to tap into additional talents within the school community. Once you get to know students, it is often relatively easy to convince them to add their voices to the choir or their skills to the jazz band or theatre production. Some students may ultimately find a bridge to traditional instruments if the door is opened to them—for instance from electric bass to double bass. The idea is to make your program accessible and appealing to your student body—to help them hone their skills and promote their interest in music—which may ultimately raise the overall profile and skill level of your entire program.

Music Appreciation

Music appreciation courses have been around for decades. However, music teachers often view teaching high school general music as a chore and do not give it the interest or attention it calls for. Yet, it is vitally important that there be options at the secondary level for students who wish to study music, but who do not have the background or interest to be involved in a performing group. The challenge for the music teacher is to create a music appreciation class that is an exciting and viable option for students—one that he or she is interested in and motivated to teach.

The key to developing an exciting course lies in the teacher's approach to planning and engaging students. General music at the secondary level can cover a wide range of music, materials, and activities: examining a variety of music and musical cultures; playing in drumming circles; learning to compose using classroom instruments or computer software and keyboards; learning to play basic chord progressions on the guitar; writing songs to be accompanied by those newly acquired guitar skills; and using piano laboratories to study ear training, harmony, and basic keyboard skills. These are just a few examples of the kinds of activities that would fit nicely into a general music class that are neither boring nor a chore.

It is important for music teachers at the secondary level to open up their programs to extend beyond performance classes and to appeal to a wider range of student skills and interests. A general music course at this level can be challenging and exciting for both teacher and students, if it is planned and implemented with the same care and consideration that is given to the performance and more advanced level theoretical courses.

Musical Theatre

School musicals are exciting and motivating events that appeal to students who are integral players in the music department, as well as those who have not been regular participants. Once the musical is over, why not keep the momentum alive by offering a musical theatre course? By doing so, you will be providing a true bridge between popular and traditional styles of music and opening up your program to students who might otherwise simply wait for the next musical to come along.

What might a musical theatre course entail? Perhaps the history of the art form; a sampling of songs or scenes from key works; and techniques for interpreting, singing, speaking, staging, and choreographing would be appropriate content. Students might prepare individual selections or work as small ensembles to prepare short scenes from various works. Selections from various musicals could make an excellent concert theme to add to the music program roster—one that would have broad appeal and likely become a favorite among the school community.

Traditional Theory and History

These may not seem like particularly progressive or even new offerings. Certainly, some schools have had traditional music courses for many years to complement their choral and instrumental offerings. Larger schools that have many students involved in private music instruction and/or many students involved in school ensembles also likely have candidates considering furthering their musical studies at the higher education level. In addition to course options for those not currently involved in music education, it is important to also consider the needs and interests of those for whom music may be a career path. Courses that offer theory will help prepare students for college music programs and significantly ease their transition from high school into more intensive music studies.

If you do not have enough students to support separate theory and history courses, you can combine them into one course that covers both areas. If you do not have enough students to support such courses, consider teaming up with a colleague in a neighboring school. Providing additional support for the music-oriented students helps strengthen their overall musicianship and their college options and entry, and reinforces your school's commitment to excellence in music education throughout the wider community.

Entry-Level Instrumental Courses

Why not offer beginning level instruction at the secondary school? Students who have not had the opportunity, or never availed themselves of the opportunity, to learn an instrument in elementary or middle school may be interested in learning to play in high school, but are rarely given the chance. If students are motivated to do so, they can progress quite quickly at this stage—potentially joining or forming an ensemble later in the year or the next one.

If you don't have the instruments at your school to supply the class, make arrangements with a local music dealer for reasonably priced rentals, as many elementary schools do. You might start with a class for one particular instrument—say, a saxophone class, and add more as interest grows. You may find that students who are currently involved in music will also be interested in the course as a means of learning a new instrument. Such a course again broadens the potential of music education in your school to reach all students—or at least all who are interested.

World Music

World music often forms a component of general music classes, but can also work effectively as individual classes at the middle and high school levels. African drumming, Mexican mariachi, and Caribbean steel bands are examples of world music offerings that have enjoyed success in various parts of the United States and might be included in your roster. Other places have found traditional Celtic music appealing to students, and bluegrass groups are alive and well in others. Such programs have grown largely out of a need to bridge gaps between traditional music education and the interests of specific cultures that are predominant in a given school community—often in urban and rural schools.

What is the cultural makeup of your school? Is there a dominant culture through whose music you could reach and engage students? Starting a new program may involve additional study on your part of the particular music, but it could open the music room door to many students who might otherwise stay away. Once engaged in music education through study of a familiar music, and once students get to know you, it is a relatively easy step to engage them in another component of your program.

Students in Financial Need

This is always a tricky subject. How do you let students know that financial support is available for them to participate in music education options, and encourage students who need the help to take advantage of it without offending their pride? I suggest that you make sure your guidance counselor, principal, secretaries, and colleagues know about financial support through a written notice and verbally at a staff meeting. While students may not feel comfortable approaching the teacher directly involved (i.e., you), they might mention it—even in passing—to a colleague. It is important for those individuals to have information to provide to students in order to make the process easier for them.

What do students need to do in order to gain financial assistance? Whom do they need to talk with about this? In some cases, it might be easier for them to discuss it with the guidance counselor and let him or her make the necessary arrangements. You might also encourage your colleagues to let you know of anyone who may be avoiding courses they are interested in due to costs.

Convincing the Unconverted

How do you go about convincing students to take a music class when they are focusing intently on the math/science "need-to-get-into-a-good-college" model? This can be tricky, and you will probably never convince everyone. But, you can influence some students' and parents' thinking about music and the arts if you take a proactive approach. First of all, colleges and employers alike value well-rounded individuals. Students who are seen to excel academically and also participate in the arts are particularly good candidates. Music education encourages those highly valued critical thinking skills that help students to succeed in college and career.

So, how do you get this information to the unconverted student? The first step is to find any information you can on the value of the arts in education—newspaper and journal articles in particular—and post them in a prominent place on your music notice board. Keep your eye open for new articles and especially materials about prominent individuals who emphasize the value that an education in the arts had on their life and success. The MENC website has recorded public service announcements from music celebrities on the value of music education and what it has meant to them. (Visit www.menc.org and search for "PSAs.") Ask your students to bring clippings that they find, too. You might also post a particularly eye-catching title in another prominent place in the school (like outside the main office).

The next thing you will want to do is talk to the guidance counselor about your program, your approach to music education, and the variety of options that are available to students. And make copies of interesting articles for him or her. If you can gain support of people in a position to influence student choices, this can be very helpful to your cause.

Another way to influence the community's thinking about music education and higher education is to include information about the music program's alumni or graduating students (particularly those who have been accepted to recognized colleges and universities) in the all-school newsletter and website. Informing the school community about recent higher education achievements of students from your music program brings home the message that students can participate in music education and be successful in the college admission process—the two are not mutually exclusive.

Promotion of Entire Program

Performing ensembles are typically promoted as hallmarks of the music department. However, if you want to build student interest in and respect for the other components of your program, you may need to raise their profile as well.

In your department newsletter make note of special projects and achievements of these classes—what they have been up to during the term. It is also important to try to include all your students in concerts in either a performing or nonperforming capacity. Your elementary music classes can perform as an Orff ensemble, present a musical play, or sing a medley. Your middle school guitar students can perform as a full class or small ensemble or they can collaborate with the middle school choir on a song or two. Your senior music appreciation students can take care of backstage management, recording, or ushering; they can work on the program and even provide program notes.

By acknowledging the efforts and achievements of all your students, you will show the students and the school community the value that you place on all components of your program. Additionally, you will raise awareness in the community of the diversity of your program.

BUILDING SKILLS

Music Conservatory

One way of encouraging students to improve their instrumental or vocal skills is to offer in-house individual instruction. Consider opening your school doors and clientele to independent music teachers. Reserve a few music rooms, practice rooms, or classrooms for after-school music lessons. Recruit university music students or other independent music teachers to teach at the school one or more days a week, and establish a common fee among teachers. Send a notice home to parents that you will be offering private instruction, making sure to include information about instruments, days, and hours. Point out the great opportunity this is for students to learn a new instrument or to hone their skills on their ensemble instrument or voice without having to leave the school.

Many parents who had not previously considered private lessons will find this an appealing option. Since the lessons take place at school, no extra picking up and driving elsewhere is required. Even if there is a gap between the last school class and the beginning of the lesson, this is time that the student can use to work on homework (if there is a library on-site or homework or afterschool support available) or practice in a safe and supervised environment. You may even find that some children who had already been studying elsewhere will begin taking lessons at the school instead because of the convenience.

If the principal is willing and there are rooms available, you can even run lessons throughout the school day as a pull-out program, with teachers following a rotating schedule so that students do not miss the same class every week. As with all new endeavors, especially one that involves outside staff, you will want to discuss the details with your principal before setting up this type of program. He or she may have concerns or wish to provide guidelines as to the method of selecting teachers for hire, how students are assigned to teachers, how much is charged for on-site lessons, whether a room or equipment rental fee is required, and the potential need for references and official background checks.

Developing a conservatory system can be a great way to raise the profile of music in your school as well as to raise your students' musical skills. Once teachers and space have been reserved, the day-to-day running of the program actually requires very little effort on your part. You can collect completed registration forms and assign students to teachers; however, the details requiring communication with parents (such as lesson times) can be taken on by the individual teachers. Do be sure to set up guidelines regarding school policy on missed lessons and payment procedures and send them home with all participating students.

You might want to arrange for billing to be done through the school, with the school issuing a check to the individual teachers. This way you can make sure that things are regulated and standardized for all teachers and students. The easiest way for the school accountant to manage this is if lessons are paid for at the beginning of each semester. Alternatively, you may wish to let individual teachers arrange their own billing. Again, these are start-up issues that should be discussed with your principal. For the minimal effort required, this type of system can increase the level of one-on-one attention given to your students, raise their level of playing, and make music even more of a presence in your school.

Ensembles in Young Grades

Children often begin violin and piano lessons at the onset of their school years. While starting private instruction this young may not necessarily be an advantage over starting a little later in elementary school, it is certainly not necessary to wait for middle or high school, as is the case in some schools, to begin instrumental instruction in school. By doing so, you may be losing valuable years of learning. Instrumental ensembles can begin successfully by fifth grade; choral ensembles can begin by third grade (some teachers may prefer to begin even younger, but by third grade most children can accurately match pitch), especially if students have had a solid general music program through elementary school.

There are a number of reasons for starting young. First of all, children in grades three to five are eager to learn new things and to be involved in group activities. Choir, band, and string ensembles are exciting options—elementary school children are eager to practice and attend rehearsals. You can use this enthusiasm to hook the children on ensemble participation early so that their skills grow and group cohesion is well developed prior to high school. This will allow them to play higher-level and potentially more musically satisfying works than they could as older beginners. As well, with well-developed skills students will be better prepared for more specialized ensembles and a greater range of musical styles.

Secondly, the later you leave it the more likely it will be that students become involved with many other activities and, although they would like to be involved in music, they simply can't find the time. Starting ensemble participation earlier helps to avoid this potential pitfall.

THE TEACHER

The Model

Beginning teachers often make the mistake of trying to be friends with their students, particularly at the high school level. This can result in a situation whereby students fail to see the line between teacher and comrade, and those teachers can have a difficult time getting students to work effectively. This situation can be a particular challenge for young teachers whose experiences, at twenty-three to twenty-four years of age, are closer to those of their students than to their older colleagues. And while it is certainly important for students to like and relate to you, it is essential that they respect you as a teacher with knowledge and experience that they do not yet have.

By maintaining a professional student-teacher relationship, your expectations of students and your ability to fairly assess their achievement will be more easily set in place. Without these components, your potential for developing a strong successful program will be severely restricted, no matter how much the kids like you. Remember that you are the musician-teacher model that your students will work to emulate. Many music education students set their sights on becoming like their former teacher. As such, you need to be ever cognizant of your behavior, attitudes, and opinions, and means of interacting with others in the school environment.

SUMMARY

Music plays an important role in most of our lives. Without it, life would be much duller in a great many capacities. Young people are not oblivious to the importance of music, but tend rather to have deep attachments and responses to it. An important part of the music teacher's job is to create a program that appeals to the musician in all students, not just those who are drawn to the traditional ensembles. While these are the backbone of most music programs, they do not tap into the interests of all students. Providing a diverse program and promoting all components of the program, building and documenting skills through early and individual instruction, and recognizing student success will ensure that music education in the school setting is truly for all students.

ASSIGNMENTS

1. Using curriculum guides for your province or state (or the National Standards for Music Education), develop course outlines for two grades that you would give to students/parents on the first day of class. Include details pertaining to course content, required materials, and assessment strategies.
2. Look into your provincial or state requirements regarding the fine and performing arts. Are courses in the arts required in elementary schools? High schools? For graduation? Poll middle and high schools in your area regarding the composition of overall averages. Is music included?
3. Discuss the feasibility of starting a new guitar class at your school. How many guitars would you need? How would you acquire them? Look into special rates that instrument manufacturers or distributors may provide for multiple purchases for a school program. Which school grades would you develop your program for? Why?
4. Discuss the expansion of your high school program to include a diverse array of courses. In addition to traditional ensembles, what courses would you choose to offer that would appeal to a broader range of students? Why?
5. Create a plan for promoting the less visible music classes in your school. How will you bring these courses and students to the attention of the school community?
6. Develop a strategy for beginning a conservatory program at your school. Which instruments will you include? How will you convince

the principal and/or governing board to agree to your plans? Draw up a plan including which school rooms might be available for use either during or after school hours. What will the most popular instrument be? Which instruments would you consider essential to offer at such a program?

Chapter 6

Publicity

Music education is an area that is easily overlooked and often misunderstood by students, parents, and administrators. Without making a conscious and continuous effort to let people see and hear about the events, achievements, and contribution of the program you work so hard to build, your students and your efforts may remain unsung. Publicly bringing music education to the school and wider community's attention is an important aspect of developing a strong program. Awareness is the key to understanding and valuing. This chapter focuses on ways to publicize your program.

VISUAL AIDS

Photos

One point that I have attempted to make throughout this book is that very often the only person in a given school who truly knows what music education is about is the music teacher. While there may be some general concept of band, orchestra, and choral classes due to their public visibility in performances, other music classes are a different story.

General music is a prime example—there may be a general idea that students sing, listen to classical music, and perhaps learn to read music. However, it is unlikely that many parents, teachers, and administrators are fully aware of the breadth and depth of learning that typically takes place. Some adults in the school community may also have biased, negative attitudes about music education, which typically stem from their own history of a weak music education or lack of one altogether. The music teacher needs to work toward dispelling myths and enlightening the community about the exciting educational programs he or she offers.

One way of getting the information out is to post images from your classes. Take your camera to class with you—carry it around for a day and snap some photos of the students in action. Then post a cross-section of these photos on your bulletin board. Visuals of students composing, playing xylophones and drums, enjoying musical games and dances, or creating listening maps or musical theatre productions can go a long way toward opening parents' eyes to the exciting, challenging, educational, and important activities that comprise their children's music education. Understanding more about what their children are doing and learning in music is the key to parents' valuing and supporting of your school program.

Note: Be sure to check with your school principal before photographing or videotaping students for any purpose. Some schools have strict policies about this. It may not be permitted or you may be required to get parental consent.

A Bulletin Board

Every music teacher needs a large, visible space on which to promote and administer various components of the music program. A large bulletin board positioned in the hallway outside the music room can be used to promote activities and performances, advocate for music education, and serve as a notice board for music students. In addition, a section of the bulletin board should be reserved for advertising musical events both in the school and in the community.

Ask local performing ensembles, halls, and promoters to put you on their mailing lists for upcoming performances. Keep this section as current as possible and make a point of mentioning upcoming events to your students. This can be done formally at the beginning or end of classes, or informally to individuals or small groups of students for whom the performance might be particularly relevant.

By encouraging your students to become concertgoers, you will broaden their perspective on musical performance (people do make their living in this profession!), support music making on a community level, encourage lifelong music patrons, and open your students' ears to high-quality music that may motivate them toward improved tone, technique, and commitment to practice. And any improvements on an individual basis will ultimately reflect the overall quality of your ensembles and your program as a whole.

The School Webpage

More and more schools have their own websites these days. Many, in particular private institutions, use them as promotional tools. And while many people think of strong math and science departments when defining a "good" school, what administrators know is that, given that the three "Rs" are relatively equal across schools, it is the arts and athletic programs that ultimately make the sale with students and parents.

Bearing this in mind, you need to ensure that photos of your performances and/or classes are available and uploaded onto your school webpage. Highlight ensemble and individual achievements, as well as special or unique aspects of your program (guitar classes, sound recording facilities, etc.). Using the Internet can help in building awareness among current students and inspire the musically inclined to choose your school, which will ultimately result in a stronger program and solid reputation.

Yearbook

Yearbook photos of the music department typically include formal pictures of performing groups. It is a good idea to also incorporate informal action shots of both classes and ensembles. And ask that several pages be dedicated to the music department. Remember that many pages will be devoted to the athletic teams, so there is no reason why your extensive program should not have a few as well. This will allow you to assemble a collection of photos of students participating in all the diverse components of your program.

Images of competitions, classes, concerts, musicals, tours, foyer performances, community performances, and retreats are powerful and long-lasting reminders of the breadth and strength of the program. Having a number of pages devoted to the music department allows you to highlight its importance in school life. Including a variety of photos from many areas of the program at various events and venues gives people a sense of its extensiveness. Seeing plenty of fun, interesting, and exciting photos of your students in action may even inspire new additions to your student roster.

Newsletters

If you want people to know what's happening in your department, you have to inform them. A few times each year—perhaps at the beginning of each semester—compile a report of the various activities of your classes and ensembles in an attractive newsletter to send home to parents. Keep each item brief and to the point so that people will be more inclined to read them.

Note students' recent achievements—the grade four's xylophone compositions, the middle school choir's performance at a senior citizen's home, and the Battle of the Bands competition. Highlight upcoming events—festival participation, the beginning of sectional rehearsals, and auditions for a new stage band. Promote performances. Let parents know when and where they can buy tickets for the school revue, big-band night, or musical.

Discuss any fund-raising efforts—what the funds will be used for, how they are to be raised, and what the anticipated goal is. Note the new guitars that were recently purchased with support from the PTA, the local music store, private donations, or last year's fund-raising. Let parents know how the guitars are being used to enhance your program. Don't forget to applaud individual student achievements and to thank parents, teachers, and administrators who have made a particular contribution to the department.

If your school already has an all-school newsletter, it is a good idea to either include the music newsletter here as an insert or write a short article for the school newsletter while sending your music department letter out at an earlier or later date (this increases the likelihood that the information you carefully put together is actually read). The more people know about what's going on in your department, the better it will be in terms of the overall music profile and status within the school community.

The Newspapers

Most newspapers have a section chronicling local events. If you have a big event coming up or currently under way, consider placing a call to your local paper. These stories have to be initiated somewhere, and you might as well be the one to get the ball rolling. No guarantee that it will work out on this particular occasion, but it certainly never hurts to let them know what your department is up to. They may ask you to send a photo and some details about the event, or they may send someone to cover it (be sure to reserve seating and provide complimentary tickets). Also, be sure to find out if an article can be written by a member of the school community. Ask about deadlines and requirements for inclusion in the community events section. An article and/or picture in the newspaper will give your program instant recognition and will be seen as a big success for the music department.

Artwork

You may not be able to make your department's presence known aurally on a daily basis; however, a visual reminder can fill in the gaps between live musical experiences. If your elementary students have been working on musical maps or invented notation, had a recent trip to the symphony, or are learning about the instruments of the orchestra; if your first-grade students have been painting images to illustrate the mood of musical selections; if your fifth-graders have been notating (graphically or traditionally) their own compositions—post this work in the hallway outside the music room. Make a sign to indicate what the artwork represents and be sure to have students sign their own pieces so that parents can easily identify them. Posting students' work is an excellent way of both keeping parents abreast of what is happening in class and serving as a visual reminder of the musical presence in the school.

Murals

Invite your students to help create a mural for your music room or for the hallway outside your music room. You may want to work according to a certain theme or perhaps let each student involved have a part of the mural that they can design as they wish. Use primed wood or canvas as the base since these are durable and long-lasting materials. Acrylic paint is a good choice for student use—it looks great, is easy to work with, and dries quickly. You might even invite the art teacher to help coordinate the effort, the purpose of which is to create a permanent monument to music education—something by the students and for the students. Murals can have a strong impact on those who see them. They are not only artistic and attention grabbing, they also represent a positive and enduring presence of music in your school.

Announcement of Achievements

Many talented young musicians work on their craft in the privacy of their own homes without much public ado about their achievements. Keep track of who the musicians are in your school. You may have to do a little investigative work to find out, especially if they are not involved in any aspect of your program. Encourage students to let you know when they are preparing for a competition, taking a conservatory exam, or giving a recital. Ask teachers to give you the heads-up on students who are away from class for musical events.

Be sure to let the school know when individuals or ensembles have made achievements in the wider community—make a congratulatory P.A. announcement or recognize the student in the school newsletter or assembly. If an achievement is made by a school ensemble, it is obvious that it will reflect well on your program. Perhaps less obvious is the fact that announcing musical achievements of individual students also reflects well on the music department, since it contributes to the overall impression of your school's success in musical endeavors. It also shows that you are a supportive music educator, regardless of who has prepared students for their successes.

LET THEM IN

An Attractive Room

This one is rather simple in theory, but much less simple in reality. A typical school day often involves a variety of equipment being moved from place to place in a music, choral, orchestra, or band room—instruments, sheet music, books, stands, chairs, valve oil, and reeds, for example. Without careful maintenance and guidelines for students, your room could easily look chaotic by the time the day is over.

Unfortunately, the end of the school day is the very time that people are most likely to pass by your space and catch a glimpse of what is inside. It is very important that they do not see chaos. If your room is messy and disorganized it can give the impression that you and your program are messy and disorganized, instead of strong and thriving (even though it is often the case that your space is messiest when things are going well and you have little time for tidying).

A neat and orderly room with instruments and books in designated places, chairs and stands neatly laid out or stacked, old reeds and scrap paper in the bin, and lost odds and ends in a box labeled "lost and found" goes a long way toward projecting an image of a teacher and program that are on top of their game. The easiest way to ensure a tidy room is to end each class a couple of minutes early so that the students can participate in cleaning things up for the next class. They may be much less likely to mess it up in the first place if they know they will ultimately be responsible for its tidying.

Aside from the day-to-day materials, it is a good idea to keep a regular check on your wall paraphernalia (posters, fingering charts, pictures, etc.). Are posters getting a little rough around the edges? Missing staples? Have they been up so long that they've lost their impact? Keeping your room looking vibrant and fresh is so important. Be sure to remove or update any materials that are past their best-before date.

At the elementary level, many teachers have children remove their shoes and place them neatly against the wall upon entering the room. (If you share your classroom with other classes, you might also ask them to remove their shoes.) Children can track a lot of dirt from the playground outside to the music room floor. Not only does this make the floors dirty, which takes away from the appearance of the space, it also makes it difficult to have children sit or do movement activities on the floor—they will either leave your class with dirt on their clothes or they will have to sit in chairs during class, which is not ideal for many elementary music activities. A simple check-your-shoes-at-the-door rule can keep the room and the students clean.

Open-Door Policy

So many people walk through school corridors during the course of the day: students, parents, teachers, administrative and support staff, school board representatives, school psychologists, social workers, tutors, and special guests. Whenever possible, let them catch a glimpse of your class in action as they pass your room.

This simple gesture can help to build an understanding of music education. It gives people a chance to learn a little about what takes place in a band rehearsal in preparation for performance. It allows them to see that from the youngest age children are creating and performing music on xylophones, metallophones, and other classroom instruments. It lets the wider community know that learning guitar techniques is part of general music classes, and that music-reading skills are taught in elementary school and reinforced through fun games.

It is important for music teachers to take every opportunity to teach not only the students, but also the wider school community, about music education. With knowledge comes power, and understanding leads to support. Of course, it is not always possible to keep the door open. Sometimes the volume of sound is simply too great and having an open door will be distracting to other classes. Other times, the passing of people in the halls is too distracting for certain types of lessons. However, when it is possible, keep the door in mind as a simple, yet effective, means of promoting your program.

Arts Week

Through collaboration with your arts colleagues, you can build a week that is filled with special events to create a sense of excitement and enthusiasm for drama, art, music, and dance. Raise the idea with your colleagues and administrators in June or September and plan for an April or May event. This will give you most of the school year to plan the week and to prepare your classes and ensembles to give their best performances.

Invite special guest clinicians to work with your students. You may wish to have specialists focus on specific areas of your existing program, such as instrumental specialists for your band and orchestra students, a guest conductor or vocal coach for your choral students, or an Orff specialist for your general music classes. You might also consider offering workshops in supplemental areas that offer a broad appeal to all students—whether or not they are currently involved in the music program, such as African or Taiko drumming, Chinese or Latin dance. Throughout the week, student ensembles and soloists can be recruited to perform in prominent areas of the building before and after school each day, and possibly at lunchtime.

Opening and closing ceremonies give a sense of importance and formality to the week. You might invite special guest performers to build excitement. Invite the principal and/or superintendent to say a few words about the value of the arts programs in the school. And take a minute to update the school community on all the great things that have been happening in each arts program.

You might choose to present your final school concert during this week, instead of nearer the end of the semester (when students are tired from exams, unfocused, and counting the days until summer break). Having the performance during Arts Week leaves some time at the end of the school year for you to conclude lessons, write reports, and plan for next year. Incorporating your major school performances into Arts Week allows you to highlight your students' and overall program achievements in an arts-rich environment, thereby ending the arts year on a very positive note.

SUMMARY

Music education may be the least understood of all school programs. Parents and administrators often know little about the complex inner workings of music classes and ensembles. This lack of knowledge can result in unsupported and diminished programs. It is therefore essential that music teachers find and/or create every opportunity possible in which to inform the school community about music education. Program components must be visible on a daily basis through photos, announcements, and newsletters. An open door, Arts Week, and other events can help to educate the community about the possibilities, diversity, complexity, and value of music education in your school.

ASSIGNMENTS

1. Design a webpage that you could use to promote your school music program. If you are not proficient in creating actual webpages on the

computer, design your layout on paper that can later be translated into a webpage. What information will you include? What will you highlight?

2. How will you design your music bulletin board? What color background will you use? Why? What headings or categories will you include? When will you prepare it? Where will you find materials to post on it? How will you maintain it and keep it up to date?

3. Brainstorm ideas for Arts Week music events that will appeal both to students currently taking music classes as well as to those who are not. Draw up a schedule for the week that includes before, during, and after-school time. Take into account activities in at least two of the other arts and leave time for some regular nonarts classes.

4. Create a newsletter for parents that describes the activities and achievements of students in all your classes.

5. Develop a simple strategy for maintaining an orderly music room throughout the school day. What will the guidelines for students be? Consider strategies for each of the school levels—elementary, middle, and high school.

6. Research recent findings on extra-musical benefits of music instruction. Which, if any, of these findings are you likely to use in promoting your program? Discuss the pros and cons of this area of research.

Chapter 7

Final Thoughts

Building a strong music program is a complex task that requires the teacher to wear many hats. For the beginning teacher, the bridge between the knowledge and skills attained in college and the real-world skills needed in their role as music teacher can seem vast and, at times, overwhelming. It is hoped that this book helps to ease the transition from college back to school for many young music teachers. Understanding that you do not need to stand alone in your quest to build a great program is a crucial hurdle to get past. The sooner you implement strategies for bringing supporters onboard, the sooner your program will grow in the way you envision.

Keeping students at the core of your vision will help to guide many of the steps you take, the courses you implement, the performances you plan, and the overall structure and direction of your program. Ultimately, music education is for students, so the needs of the entire student body need to be constantly considered and, hopefully, met through a diverse, engaging, organized, and high-quality program. Getting the word out about your program is key and continuous. Everyday promotion of the school music program is as essential a component of building and maintaining a strong program as developing exceptional courses and performances.

The music education profession is a rewarding one. Music is such a powerful force in people's lives—being able to create and understand music is indeed a gift that students cherish long after their school days are over. And teachers are in the somewhat daunting position of, every day, being able to affect people's lives, for better or for worse. Many people, in all sorts of professions, recall with fondness the impact that participation in music education had on their lives. As a music teacher, you are part of a select group of individuals who can bring both immediate and lifelong joy and learning to a vast number of people—thousands over the course of a career. What an amazing contribution to life—one that few other professions can claim. My sincere best wishes on your journey to create strong, vibrant, joyful, and lasting music programs!

Appendix

SELECTED RESOURCES

The following associations, websites, publishers, and books are invaluable resources for the new music educator. Topics included are those discussed throughout the book that frequently do not receive great depth in college music education courses, yet are essential topics for teachers at all levels.

Advocacy

Coalition for Music Education in Canada (coalitionformusiced.ca/
html/sec4-advocacy/publications.php)
MENC (www.menc.org/resources/view/music-education-advocacy
-central)
Music For All (www.musicforall.org/resources/advocacy/panic.aspx)
Support Music (NAMM and MENC) (www.supportmusic.com)
VH1 Save the Music (www.vh1.com/partners/save_the_music)

Assessment

Brophy, T. S. (2000). *Assessing the Developing Child Musician: A Guide for Music Teachers*. Chicago: GIA.
Farrell, S. (2000). *Tools for Powerful Student Evaluation*. Galesville, MD: Meredith Music.
MENC (1996). *Performance Standards for Music Grades PreK12: Benchmarks for Assessing Progress toward the National Standards*. Reston, VA: MENC.

Associations

American Choral Directors Association (www.acdaonline.org)
American Orff Schulwerk Association (www.aosa.org)
American School Band Directors Association (home.comcast.net/
  ~asbda/)
American String Teachers Association (www.astaweb.com)
Canadian Band Association (www.canadianband.ca)
Canadian Music Educators' Association/L'Association canadienne des
  musiciens éducateurs (www.cmea.ca)
Carl Orff Canada: Music for Children (www.orffcanada.ca)
Dalcroze Society of America (www.dalcrozeusa.org)
International Society for Music Education (ISME) (www.isme.org)
Kodály Society of Canada (www.kodalysocietyofcanada.ca)
MENC: The National Association for Music Education (www.menc.org)
MENC State Chapters (www.menc.org/about/view/menc-state-
  affiliates)
National Association for Gifted Children (www.nagc.org)
Organization of American Kodály Educators (OAKE) (www.oake.org)
Technology Institute for Music Educators (www.ti-me.org)
Tri-M Music Honor Society (www.menc.org/resources/view/tri-m-music
  -honor-society-tri-m-overview)

Classroom Management

Haugland, S. L. (2007). *Crowd Control: Classroom Management and Effective
  Teaching for Chorus, Band, and Orchestra.* Lanham, MD: MENC/Rowman
  & Littlefield Education.
Moore, M., Batey, L. B., and Royse, D. M. (2002). *Classroom Management in
  General, Choral, and Instrumental Music Programs.* Reston, VA: MENC.

Copyright and Mechanical Licensing

Althouse, J. (1999). *Copyright: The Complete Guide for Music Educators.* Van
  Nuys, CA: Alfred.
Harry Fox Agency (www.harryfox.com)
MENC Copyright Center (www.menc.org/resources/view/copyright
  -center)

Exceptional Students

Adamek, M. and Darrow, A.-A. (2005). *Music in Special Education.* Silver
  Spring, MD: American Music Therapy Association.

Gregory, G. and Chapman, C. (2001). *Differentiated Instructional Strategies: One Size Doesn't Fit All*, 2nd ed. Thousand Oaks, CA: Corwin Press.

Robinson, A., Shore, B., and Emerson, D. (2007). *Best Practices in Gifted Education: An Evidence-Based Guide*. Waco, TX: Prufrock Press.

Sobel, E. S. (2008). *An Attitude and Approach for Teaching Music to Special Learners*. Lanham, MD: MENC/Rowman & Littlefield Education.

Multicultural Music Education

Campbell, P. (2004). *Teaching Music Globally: Experiencing Music, Expressing Culture*. New York: Oxford University Press.

Nettl, B., Capwell, C., Wong, I. K. F, and Turino, T. (2004). *Excursions in World Music*, 4th ed. Upper Saddle River, NJ: Prentice Hall.

Titon, J. (2004). *World of Music: An Introduction to the Music of the World's People, Shorter Version*, 2nd ed. Belmont, CA: Schirmer/Thompson.

Wade, B. C. (2004). *Thinking Musically: Experiencing Music, Expressing Culture*. New York: Oxford University Press.

See also Rowman & Littlefield Education/MENC (in the "Publishers" section below) for a variety of practical publications on starting up specific world music ensembles. To learn about the music of a specific country or region, see the excellent Global Music Series by Oxford University Press.

Publishers

The following publishers print books about all facets of music education. They are excellent sites for teacher resources (enter *music education* as the search term):

GIA (www.giamusic.com)
Meredith Music (meredithmusic.com)
Oxford University Press (www.oup.com/us)
Prentice-Hall (www.pearsonhighered.com)
Rowman & Littlefield Education (copublishers with MENC) (www.romaneducation.com)
Thompson Higher Education (www.cengage.com/wadsworth)

About the Author

Charlene Ryan is assistant professor of music education at the Berklee College of Music in Boston. She was formerly chair of music education at McGill University in Montreal, Canada. She holds degrees from the University of Western Ontario, the University of Michigan, Memorial University, and McGill University. Before moving into higher education, Professor Ryan was the preschool–middle school music teacher at West Point Grey Academy in Vancouver, Canada. She has taught general, choral, and instrumental music at all school levels from pre-K to grade twelve. In addition, Dr. Ryan developed a very successful community music education program for young children in Montreal and codirects Berklee's popular Kids Jam program for preschool age children in Boston. She is the past-president of the Quebec Music Educators Association.

In addition to her interest in developing strong and lasting music programs, Dr. Ryan engages in research studies on the performance experiences of young musicians. In 2005 she was awarded a $130,000 grant from the Social Sciences and Humanities Research Council of Canada to study the development and experience of performance anxiety in children and adolescents. She has published in the *Journal of Research in Music Education*, the *International Journal of Research in Music Education*, *Psychology of Music*, the *International Journal of Stress Management*, *Medical Problems of Performing Artists*, and *Teaching Music*. She lives in the Boston area with her husband and two young sons.